Stammering

A Practical Guide for
Teachers and Other Professionals

**Lena Rustin, Frances Cook,
Willie Botterill, Cherry Hughes
and Elaine Kelman**

David Fulton Publishers
London

MW

David Fulton Publishers Ltd
Ormond House, 26–27 Boswell Street, London WC1N 3JZ

www.fultonpublishers.co.uk

First published in Great Britain by David Fulton Publishers 2001

British Library Cataloguing in Publication Data
A catalogue record for this book is available from the British Library

ISBN 1-85346-714-6

The publishers would like to thank Christine Avery for copy-editing and Yvonne Messenger for proofreading this book.

Typeset by Mark Heslington, Scarborough, North Yorkshire
Printed in Great Britain by Bell and Bain Ltd, Glasgow

08/27/03

Contents

Foreword

By the time I first met her, Lena Rustin was already a legend in the world of speech therapy. After I had met her I came away convinced that the specialist work she proposed to do with children was something I not only could but should do everything to support.

The result was the Michael Palin Centre for Stammering Children which, from modest beginnings, has grown in facilities and in status. The reason for its success lies with the hard work, persistence and skill of Lena Rustin herself and the team of marvellous therapists which she has built around her, including the co-authors of this book – Frances Cook, Willie Botterill and Elaine Kelman, together with Cherry Hughes, contributing teacher. The results of their work have won great praise and given me enormous pleasure. Whenever I have seen members of the team in action I have been impressed by their concentration, patience and particularly by the rapport they seem to strike up with the children and their families, many of whom have written to me to express their gratitude for the treatment they have received at the Centre.

I know from the experience of my own father that the inability to speak fluently can be an enormous burden in life. The authors of this manual have lightened that burden for many and changed lives immeasurably for the better. I am proud to be associated with them and delighted that this book gives teachers and other professionals the chance to learn from their experience and hopefully share in their success. We know the scale of the problem and there is a desperate need for greater understanding of the disability and how to manage it. Hard-pressed teachers and other professionals have a crucial role to play if we are to succeed in the enormous task of restoring dignity and respect to those affected by stammering.

Michael Palin
May 2001

Dedication

This book is dedicated to all the children and young adults who stammer, and their families, who have been to the Michael Palin Centre – they have inspired us and without them we would not have been able to write this book.

Acknowledgements

The authors would like to thank the following people who contributed so much to the contents of this book with their knowledge, time, encouragement and support:

The speech and language therapists at the Michael Palin Centre, who assisted with the contents of the book: Alison Nicholas, Jane Fry, Sharon Millard, Julie Hunt, and Ali Biggart.

Diana de Grunwald and Patricia Brown for their help in correcting the manuscript.

Michael Palin for his generous foreword to the book and his commitment to the Centre.

The Board of the Association for Research into Stammering in Childhood for all their support.

The British Stammering Association for their interest and encouragement.

All the families of the authors for their patience and support.

Introduction

This book is primarily intended for those who work in schools, including head teachers, class teachers, special educational needs coordinators (SENCOs) and learning support assistants (LSAs). We have used the label 'teacher' in the generic sense to apply to all school staff who work directly on the education of children. We also hope that this book will prove a useful resource for parents who are concerned about their child who stammers in school. In addition it may be helpful for opening a dialogue about stammering between speech and language therapists and teachers.

Collaboration between services is being emphasised in recent government documents, papers and policies and we do accept that this should be a priority. We are very aware of the classroom demands that are made on teaching staff generally and the range of skills that they need to acquire to help children with identified Special Educational Needs. The message that we hope to convey is that there are some relatively straightforward principles that would support not only children who stammer but also others with a range of communication difficulties.

Stammering is not very common; it is complex, variable and unpredictable. There are different factors that contribute to each child's problem and affect how the stammer develops. This makes it hard to offer unequivocal advice, as strategies that help one child may be counterproductive for another. This accounts for some of the anxiety that many people experience when they find themselves talking to a child who stammers, and wonder how to respond.

We aim to provide enough information about stammering for readers to appreciate the complexities of the problem but also to feel more knowledgeable and more confident in their approach to pupils and parents. Bearing in mind the enormous pressures on teachers' time, we have made the assumption that some readers will want to access the information they need quickly and easily to deal with an immediate situation while others, we hope, will be tempted to read more. As a result we occasionally found it necessary to include some items more than once.

We have attempted to explain some of the theories about the nature and causes of stammering in the first chapter. Then we give a brief overview of some speech and language therapy options that may be offered to a child and family. Following the section on speech and language therapy provision, Chapter 3 considers an educational perspective and the difficulties the child who stammers may face in school. The next three chapters offer practical ideas for identifying the characteristics of stammering in an individual pupil and practical ideas for dealing with the problem. For convenience, these chapters are divided into Early Years, Primary and Secondary although the developmental stages of stammering are often not clearly associated with chronological age.

Chapter 7 is entitled 'Social communication skills and stammering' and describes some of the techniques that we have found helpful in teaching social communication skills to clients who stammer. Given the emphasis on communication skills in education, we felt that sharing some of the practical exercises that we use might demonstrate the numerous commonalities between educational and speech and language therapy goals.

Throughout the text we have used the masculine pronoun to refer to the child who stammers and the feminine for the clinician, partly because this makes it easier to read but also because it reflects the fact that the majority of people who stammer are male and their therapists are mainly female.

The Appendices are full sized versions of figures that can be photocopied for use within your school.

In the final section we have supplied some useful contacts and their addresses.

Chapter 1

What is stammering?

Introduction

Stammering occurs in all parts of the world, across all cultures, religions and socioeconomic groups, as well as in all languages and at all levels of intelligence. It is a complex problem, which has confounded and perplexed researchers, people who stammer and their relatives, throughout time. It is a disorder where even the name creates confusion as it may be referred to as stammering, stuttering and/or dysfluency, all of which refer to the same problem.

Throughout this book we have used stammering to describe the problem, except when discussing the emergence and early development of children's difficulties with fluency; these we refer to as dysfluencies in recognition of the numbers of children who have a transient period of difficulty and then recover.

Stammering varies from individual to individual and from day to day. This can often result in bewilderment and frustration, not only for the person who is stammering, but for the listener as well. There is a great deal that we still do not know about stammering, including its underlying causes and the most successful methods of treating it. What has become increasingly clear is that for each individual, stammering is the result of a combination of different factors and that its effect varies from person to person.

This chapter will focus on what we do know about stammering – what it is, what behaviours are typical, the reasons why one child's fluency is more vulnerable than another's and the impact that this disorder may have upon a child. There are a number of questions which families and professionals frequently ask about the nature and development of stammering, and these will be discussed in the light of current research findings and illustrated by two useful theoretical models.

What is stammering?

It may be helpful to start with a definition. Guitar (1998) puts it simply as 'an abnormally high frequency or duration of stoppages in the forward flow of speech. These stoppages usually take the form of (a) repetitions of sounds, syllables, or one-syllable words, (b) prolongations of sounds, or (c) "blocks" of airflow or voicing in speech. Children are usually aware of the problem and embarrassed by it, and it is frequently associated with excessive physical and mental effort'. (p. 10)

One of the difficulties in trying to describe stammering is that it varies so much from individual to individual, in terms of the type of behaviours present and the frequency with which they occur. There are however some features which are typically characteristic of stammering:

- Repetition of whole words, e.g. 'and, and, and, then I left.'
- Repetition of single sounds, e.g. 'c-c-come here.'
- Prolongation of sounds, e.g. 'sssssssometimes I go out.'
- Blocking of sounds, where the mouth is in position but no sound comes out.
- Facial tension – excessive muscular tension may be evident, for instance, around the eyes, nose, lips or neck.
- Concomitant movements – extra body movements may occur as the child attempts to 'push' the word out. Examples include: stamping the feet, shifting body position or tapping with the hands.
- The breathing pattern may be disrupted, for example, the child may hold his breath while speaking, speak while breathing in, or take an exaggerated breath before speaking.

Whatever the particular features are, the flow of speech is interrupted and may cause considerable distress to the speaker and the listener. In addition, the child may adopt strategies in order to minimise the problem – these are quite easy to miss and may include:

- Avoidance of words – a child may react to an imminent stammering episode by avoiding or changing the 'difficult' word. For instance, a child may suddenly, 'forget what he was going to say', or change a word which he begins to stammer on: e.g. 'I played with my br, br, br, (brother) . . . sister on Saturday'. At times this can change the meaning of the child's utterance and may cause confusion or even bewilderment on the part of the listener!
- Avoidance of situations – some children respond to their difficulty by avoiding talking to certain people or talking in certain situations. While it isn't true for all children who

stammer, it is quite common for children to describe how they avoid speaking in assembly or answering questions in class.

Some children become so adept at hiding their problem in this manner that they may *appear* fluent, or *become very quiet*.

- Variability – one of the most difficult features to understand or explain about stammering is its variability. The problem can fluctuate from mild to severe depending on the situation. It is different for each person, and may range from whole and part word repetitions a few times a day for one child, to blocking for 3–4 seconds, accompanied by foot stamping and facial contortions on nearly every other word for another. It can change from hour to hour and day to day. Parents will often report that a child has been fluent for several days or even weeks only to begin stammering again without warning. This is one of the features of stammering that makes it such a difficult problem to respond to, since what is appropriate one day may change the next.

When does it begin?

It is generally agreed that stammering may occur at any time during childhood but it usually starts between the ages of two and five years (Andrews *et al*. 1983).

How does it start?

It frequently emerges gradually, although it can also begin very suddenly, and often during a period of rapid expansion of speech and language skills.

Who is affected?

Approximately five per cent of all children will experience some difficulty with their fluency at some time during the development of their speech. The vast majority of these children will achieve normal fluency, with or without some help. However, for some, complete fluency is not attainable and around one per cent of the adult population stammers (Bloodstein 1995). Unfortunately, determining which children are likely to regain fluency and which are more likely to persist in stammering is problematic. Current research, however, continues to provide us with new findings and information that assist with this.

Research indicates that, at onset, there are nearly as many girls who stammer as boys, but that this picture changes over time. Girls begin stammering a little earlier and are more likely to overcome the problem than boys (Yairi *et al*. 1992). By the age of ten, the ratio of boys to girls who stammer can be as high as 5:1 (Bloodstein 1995).

How are people affected?

The experience of being unable to speak affects children in different ways. Some are not very aware or concerned while others are extremely anxious and worried about it. The degree of concern that the child has in relation to speech does not necessarily correlate with the frequency or severity of the stammer. Children may experience feelings of frustration at not being able to get the words out as quickly as they wish. Feelings of embarrassment and shame may also accompany speaking, particularly if a child has experienced negative responses or teasing from others. These unhelpful feelings associated with speech can increase the child's anxiety and tension in talking situations which can, in turn, make the stammering worse.

Over time these feelings can also affect the child's self-esteem and self-image. Not only can the child's confidence in the ability to speak fluently be reduced, but confidence in social inter-actions and everyday activities generally can also be lost. Those who feel confident about themselves generally, who are able to develop strategies to enhance communication and maximise fluency, and who can utilise effective problem solving skills, are more likely to be able to approach and manage difficult situations positively.

How does stammering change through childhood?

As children get older, their skills and capacities will increase, but so will the demands placed on them. The child will grad-ually be exposed to a wide range of life experiences, and encounter increasingly diverse speaking situations. Each of these will have an effect on the child's growing awareness of himself and the response and perceptions of others to his stammering. In addition, the frequency and/or severity of the stammer will fluctuate, either in association with these changes, or in spite of them. The following chapters will discuss the developmental issues for each age group, the impact of these on the child's fluency and the vital role teachers have in supporting the child in the classroom.

There are a number of questions that are frequently asked by parents, teachers and children which have their roots in misconceptions, old wives' tales, inaccurate professional opinions and out of date research.

Some questions that are frequently asked about stammering

Q. *Children go through a phase of stammering and grow out of it, don't they?*

A. *Well – yes and no!*

As mentioned above, it is true that many children pass through a period of dysfluency that may last several weeks, or even months, and then become fluent. Estimates of the numbers of children who recover spontaneously vary enormously. In a review of the studies, Bloodstein (1995) found recovery rates from 36 per cent to 79 per cent in early stammering.

The latest research suggests that higher rates of spontaneous remission are associated with

- female children;
- children who have good phonological, language and non-verbal skills;
- no family history of stammering;
- relatives who have stammered but have recovered.

Recovery is most likely to take place within 12–18 months of the onset (Yairi *et al.* 1996).

While stammering has been reported to resolve at any age, the longer a child has been stammering, the more entrenched the problem becomes (Seider *et al.* 1983). Undoubtedly, the earlier that help is provided, the more likely the child is to either overcome the problem or learn to manage it successfully. For older children, where the stammering is more likely to persist, the aims of therapy will focus on helping the individual child to develop strategies to enhance their fluency, to minimise the associated anxiety and thereby to reduce the impact that the problem has on the child's life.

Q. *Can parents cause stammering?*

A. *No*

This misconception began in the 1940s, when an American speech pathologist, Wendell Johnson, suggested that 'highly anxious' parents misdiagnosed normal dysfluencies as stammering. Furthermore it was suggested that the 'negative reactions' to their child's speech then caused the child to struggle to stop these moments of dysfluency and that it was this effort that created stammering.

Following this, there were a large number of studies that investigated whether parents of children who stammer interact differently from other parents. There is *no* evidence in any of the research literature to support this. There is *some* evidence, albeit controversial, that adults respond differently to children who stammer, such as interrupting more often and talking more quickly (Meyers and Freeman 1985 a, b). In other words parents don't do anything to cause the stammer but once it is established some parents behave differently in response to the child (Kloth *et al.* 1998).

Clinical experience has demonstrated that working with parents and carers to modify some of these behaviours, such as slowing the rate of speech and improving turn taking, are often helpful in facilitating fluency (Stephenson-Opsal and Bernstein-Ratner 1988; Langlois and Long 1988).

Q. Do people stammer because they are shy and nervous?

A. No

Studies have shown that negative stereotyping of people who stammer is widespread (Horsley and Fitzgibbon 1987). It seems that many speech and language therapists, students, teachers and parents, tend to ascribe 'negative' personality traits such as shy, nervous and insecure to people who stammer. Yet there is *no* evidence in the research to support these beliefs (Caruso *et al.*1995, Miller 1993, Weber and Smith 1990). In fact, there is exactly the same spread of personality types among people who stammer as there is in the rest of the population. It is clear that the more anxious any speaker is, the more likely they are to be dysfluent and that this is especially true for many people who stammer (Caruso *et al.* 1995, Miller 1993).

Q. Is it caused by being left handed?

A. No

In the 1920s there was a theory that stammering was caused by making left handed children write with their right hands. Eventually, after many years, the theory was properly tested and there was no evidence to support this idea.

However, there has been considerable interest over the years in the possibility that there may be a 'neurological' explanation for stammering. Recent medical, scientific, and technological advances offer us a greater understanding about the way the brain is organised for speech and language. Most speakers use the left side of the brain to process language, and recent research is investigating the possible differences between adults who stammer and those who do not. Early results appear to show that there are some differences and that people who stammer are using the right side of the brain for processing language more than fluent speakers (De Nil 1999). This could be very important for a number of reasons, including the fact that certain emotions are also processed more on the right side of the brain, and the question arises as to whether the proximity of the two sites may make fluency especially vulnerable to emotional disruption for these individuals. However, it is important to note that research so far has only been conducted on adults, so it is not possible to generalise any findings to children.

Q. *Can you catch it?*

A. *No*

Some parents have worried that their child may have 'caught' the stammering from another child or adult, or that he has copied someone in the classroom. There is no evidence in the research literature that this is the case and it would seem unlikely that children would choose to speak in this manner if they have the choice.

Q. *Could it have something to do with intelligence?*

A. *Not really*

It has often been suggested that people who stammer are either very intelligent or not very bright. The research suggests that there is no truth in either statement. People who stammer generally show the same spread of intelligence levels as the rest of the population.

However, a recent study found that non-verbal intelligence, while *still within normal limits*, was *slightly* lower among children who stammer than among a matched control group, and that higher levels of non-verbal intelligence seemed to be associated with a better chance of recovery from stuttering (Yairi *et al.* 1996).

Q. *Will it go away if you ignore it?*

A. *No – and yes!*

Many parents receive the advice to 'just ignore it' from friends and professionals. This obviously works well for those children who are going to grow out of it anyway! However, once the child is aware of the difficulties, and/or is expressing concern or frustration with his speech, this is really unhelpful.

Many children are aware of some dysfluencies from an early age, and it is not uncommon for children as young as three to describe the difficulties they are facing. Furthermore it is interesting to note that advice to ignore the problem is often contrary to the instinct of parents, who may feel the need to acknowledge the difficulty their child is experiencing. Suggestions or comments such as 'Take your time', 'There's no hurry', and 'I'm listening' can often be helpful and encouraging. Generally speaking, advising *anyone* who is anxious about something to ' just ignore it' – is usually unhelpful and often impossible.

Q. Does stammering occur on certain letters?

A. Yes – and no

Some children describe very clearly that there are certain sounds and words that they know are more difficult. While this *is* true some of the time, depending on the circumstances, there will be times when the same words or sounds are much less problematic. For some children, there are certain 'key' words that become especially difficult. For instance, children are often asked to say their names and, under the pressure of the 'spotlight', they might stammer. After this has happened a few times, they may start to associate the difficulty with the first letter, e.g. 'Mmmmmark' or 'Aaaalice'. There are no specific sounds that are more likely to result in stammering than others (Nierman *et al.* 1994). But in time children will notice sounds or words that they have stammered on, then begin to predict that they will stammer on them again, become anxious the next time and as a result are more likely to be dysfluent. This cycle can establish a self-fulfilling prophecy, but the child will often fail to notice the times that they say the word or sound without stammering.

So what does cause stammering?

There is general consensus among researchers that there is no single explanation for stammering. There are two main theoretical perspectives which help explain stammering that are widely accepted in this country, the 'Demands and Capacities Model' (Starkweather 1987) and 'multifactorial' frameworks such as the one proposed by Rustin *et al.* (1996). These view-points are complementary, each helping to explain the other, and both will be outlined below.

Starkweather developed this model as a way of understanding the forces that influence the development of fluency in children. He suggests that stammering occurs when the demands on a child's fluency exceed the child's motor, linguistic, emotional and cognitive capacity for fluent speech (Starkweather and Givens-Ackerman 1997, p. 60). Most children are born with a 'capacity' to develop speech, language and fluency skills. These 'capacities' include the child's general cognitive abilities and language formulation skills, their ability to plan, organise and control the movements for speech and their social-emotional maturity.

The 'demands' may be external and come from the child's communicative environment: for example, having to compete for a turn to talk or conversing with people who talk very quickly. The demands may also arise from the child's natural tendencies and instincts. Some children set themselves high standards, and perhaps attempt to use complex language and/or speak more quickly than they can manage. Indeed, parents often comment that their child appears 'to have a lot to say but his mouth can't keep up with his brain'. For each child the nature of this imbalance between demands and capacities is different. It may be that a child has difficulty finding the words they need quickly, reducing their capacity for fluency. Alternatively, the competition for talking space from an older, highly articulate sibling may place excessive demands on a child's fluency or indeed both may occur (Starkweather and Gottwald 1990). It is the speech and language therapist's role to assess the child's capacity for fluency and the demands being placed on those skills, and to make therapy recommendations based on these.

The Demands and Capacities Model

This framework complements the Demands and Capacities Model described above, but it also explains that for each child there will be a different combination of factors that make the developing fluency more vulnerable to disruption. These factors are grouped under four headings: physical, linguistic, environmental, and psychological (Rustin *et al.* 1996).

Factors are divided into these four categories for ease of understanding and explanation but in reality these categories are interlinked, each impacting on the others.

As is demonstrated in the diagram (Figure 1.1), some factors could be included under two or three headings. For instance, rate of speech could be considered to be either a linguistic or a physiological factor. Furthermore, speech rate may also be influenced by the child's emotional state or by the environment, increasing for instance when he is anxious, or when he is trying

A Multifactorial Framework

to keep up with other quick speakers. No single factor can be identified as the cause of an individual's stammering.

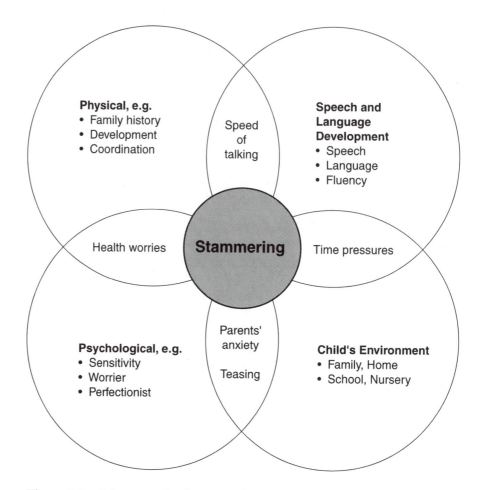

Figure 1.1 A framework of stammering

Examples of factors in each of these four groups will be presented in the following sections.

Physiological factors

Inheritance
Stammering does tend to run in families and therefore the predisposition to stammer may be inherited (Ambrose *et al.* 1993; Bloodstein 1995; Yairi *et al.* 1996). Recent research suggests that those children who have relatives who continue to stammer into adulthood have a higher chance of a persisting problem (Yairi *et al.* 1996). However, it is also quite common for a child to stammer where there are no inherited factors, so inheritance alone is not enough.

Gender

As mentioned previously, more boys stammer than girls and this sex ratio increases with age (Bloodstein 1995), indicating that girls are more likely to recover than boys.

Brain functioning research

Brain imaging is a new area of research in adults who stammer. Early findings suggest that certain aspects of language may be processed in different areas of the brain in adults who stammer (De Nil 1999). What is not yet clear is whether this is at the root of the stammering problem or a response to the difficulty with talking. Since it is not ethically possible to conduct the current experiments with children, this cannot be determined, nor can the results be generalised to the younger population. Finally, this research seems to provide further evidence that adults who stammer have particular difficulty with planning and coordinating the movements for speech.

Oral motor skills

There are a number of studies demonstrating that some children who stammer take longer to initiate speech related movements (Cullinan and Springer 1980; Till *et al.* 1983) and that people who stammer tend to have slower consonant vowel transitions and demonstrate slower speech movements generally than fluent speakers (Starkweather and Myers 1979; Zimmerman 1980). The underlying reason for this has not yet been determined but it has been proposed that some children who stammer have difficulties with the motor planning aspect of talking (Bloodstein 1995), which is now being supported by the studies mentioned earlier.

Linguistic factors

The relationship between language and stammering continues to be investigated, and research indicates that children who stammer are more likely to have other, sometimes quite subtle, difficulties with the development of their speech and language systems (Bernstein-Ratner 1997). From a developmental perspective, stammering generally emerges at a time when a child's linguistic system is undergoing a period of rapid development and it has been suggested that this dramatic increase in language skills may overload the fluency system. Stammering is also more likely to occur at the beginning of a sentence or phrase (Wall 1981) and is more frequent in longer, more grammatically complex utterances (Logan and Conture 1995).

In his discussion of the literature, Bloodstein (1995, p. 290) concludes that stammering is more likely to occur on content words (these are information carrying words, such as 'mummy') rather than function words (these are words which help link the content words together, such as 'a', 'it', 'as'). More recently a study by Howell *et al.* in 1999 suggests that when children start to stammer it occurs more on function words and as they get older they have more difficulty with content words. Finally, there are indications that children who stammer and who have additional speech sound difficulties and/or language delay are at greater risk of chronic stammering (Paden *et al.* 1999; Watkins 1999).

Social and environmental factors

As stated, parents and families do not cause a child to stammer, but the environment in which the child functions and the stressors within that environment are important. The attitudes, behaviours and events that occur at home and school will all have an impact on a child's fluency. For instance, adults may unintentionally place demands on the child to speak using complex language at a rate that is beyond the child's developmental capacity. Some children need more time than others to process and formulate speech, they also often need to speak at a slower rate in order to be fluent. This will be considerably harder to do if the people around them are talking quickly, interrupting each other and are often in a rush. Similarly, speaking situations that make a child feel anxious will often result in an increase in stammering, for example being teased or bullied, family crises, periods of difficulty or change (Guitar 1998, p. 67).

The view that the environment plays an important role in a child's development of fluency is supported by valuable clinical evidence which shows that helping families make changes in the way they respond and interact with a stammering child can result in increased fluency.

Psychological factors

It is worth repeating that while people who stammer are often assumed to be nervous, shy and anxious, the research into personality traits is clear: there is *no* evidence to suggest that there are any personality or emotional differences (Bloodstein 1995). There is some evidence that adults who stammer have more difficulty with social adjustment than their fluent peers but this is best explained as the effect of stammering on their social experience.

Oyler and Ramig (1995) found that children who stammer are more sensitive in nature than those who do not and that mothers of children who stammer rated them as significantly more sensitive than fluent children in the control group.

In addition, a heightened sensitivity towards moments of dysfluency and the listener's response may trigger an increase in physical tension, which in turn increases the likelihood of stammering. A less sensitive child may be dysfluent but remain unaffected by disruptions in their speech.

It is the role of the speech and language therapist to assess children who stammer, to identify the factors which may have made the fluency vulnerable to breakdown, to determine the factors which are significant in making it difficult for the child to establish and maintain fluency and to identify an appropriate intervention based on this knowledge.

Summary

- Stammering is characterised by whole and part word repetitions, prolongations and/or blocking of sounds. Other 'concomitant' behaviours such as stamping or blinking may also be evident.
- Children may avoid words or situations in which they anticipate stammering.
- Stammering affects approximately five per cent of children, some will recover without help, and many will recover with help.
- One per cent of children will continue to stammer into adulthood.
- More boys stammer than girls, on average 5:1 by the age of ten.
- Stammering tends to run in families; approximately 50 per cent of those who stammer also have relatives who stammer.
- The onset of stammering can be gradual or sudden and occurs between two and five years of age.
- Stammering is a complex problem; it is probably the result of a number of different factors occurring together, which predisposes a child to stammering.
- There are physiological, linguistic, environmental, and psychological factors that may contribute to the problem of stammering.

Chapter 2

Speech and language therapy

The majority of speech and language therapists (SLT) employed by the National Health Service see children with a wide range of communication problems. They may be based in hospitals, health centres, specialist units, or special schools. There are also an increasing number of services being developed within the mainstream schools where speech and language therapists are working alongside teachers. While all therapists have a similar basic training, many will develop specialist knowledge and skills for particular client groups, for example children with cleft palates, physical disabilities or hearing impairment.

Introduction

A child who stammers is most likely to be referred to the SLT department in the local health centre or, in some districts, to the speech and language therapy team who provide a service to mainstream schools. In some trusts there may also be a therapist who specialises in fluency disorders, and is available to provide additional support and expertise to colleagues, families, and schools.

The SLT service within a health centre usually offers an 'early years service' with responsibility for children up to school entry at the age of five, although this has become less clear-cut with the new programme of nursery classes attached to primary schools.

Mainstream schools SLT teams will have responsibility for children over five, and their main focus will usually be within primary schools. Each SLT service will have developed its own policies about prioritisation, and about levels and types of provision for children with and without statements of special educational needs.

This chapter aims to provide teachers with an overview of the referral and assessment procedures and then to outline the therapy process and how this may differ across different age groups.

Referring a child

Speech and language therapy is a direct access service. This means that anyone, including teachers, can, with parental permission, make a referral directly to the local SLT service. Parents, health visitors, GPs or school medical officers make referrals most frequently. Leaflets about the local service will be available from the Health Centre or the Headquarters of the Community Health Services NHS Trust or Primary Care Trusts.

Provision at the local health centre

Following a referral to a health centre, an appointment will be sent to the child's home – the timing of this can usually be negotiated with the clinic although it may require some time taken out of school. This first appointment may be called an initial 'screening'. This initial session is often considered a useful means for discerning whether the family is able to or wants to attend the clinic or, because referral information is often very sketchy, to make sure that it is a correct referral for this child.

The next step will be to arrange for the child to have a full speech and language therapy assessment. Following this, and in consultation with the parents/carers, recommendations for therapy will be made as appropriate and an action plan for liaising with other professionals who are involved will be agreed.

Provision within the school settings

Again this will vary across different services, but in some localities the SLT may, with parents' permission, see the child within the school environment and, depending on the school policy, there are a number of ways of making this visit as productive as possible.

Sometimes the child will be seen by the SLT in a one-to-one session in a quiet room, with or without the teacher or assistant, to carry out the more formal aspects of the assessment.

The therapist may then be invited to sit in with a class to gain a better understanding of the child's communication skills within this setting. Clearly the SLT would need to observe the rules and procedures for any visitor within the classroom and to arrange some other time to meet the teacher when it would be convenient to discuss the child's difficulties and, together, identify any individual curriculum needs.

Where there are therapists based within mainstream schools the procedure may be less formal in the initial stages, involving observation and consultation with parents and teachers. More formal assessments may then be conducted within the school or perhaps in conjunction with specialist services for children who stammer where these are available.

Parental involvement

Parents are key figures in the child's environment and play a crucial role in supporting and encouraging the development of their child's speech and language skills particularly in the early years. They are usually the first to notice when something is not quite 'right'. Parents frequently report their feelings of distress, confusion and helplessness when they begin to notice that their child is stammering – particularly when someone else in the family has the problem. Naturally parents want to get help for their child as soon as possible and they want to be reassured and advised about what they should be doing at home.

It is important for therapists and parents to work together from the beginning. A shared understanding of the problem, joint decision-making and an active role in helping their child is the best foundation for a successful outcome.

The assessment process

As discussed in Chapter 1 the complexity of stammering is such that each child presents with a unique set of issues. Effective therapy depends upon a detailed assessment and a treatment programme that meets the needs of the individual. The assessments used will depend on the age of the child.

The full assessment aims to provide the parents with the following:

- an opportunity to voice their worries about the problem;
- information about the factors that could have contributed to its onset and development;
- general information about stammering;
- answers to their questions;
- information on what therapy involves and what the outcome is likely to be.

The child assessment

This aims to gather information on the nature and severity of the stammering problem and how it affects the child. The speech, language and general communication skills will also be investigated to establish whether these are contributing to, or affected by, the problem.

What is the stammer like and how much is the child stammering?
The child's speech is tape-recorded during a variety of graded speaking tasks, the sample will be analysed for particular characteristics and a measure of the percentage of stammering is calculated to give some idea of the range and severity of the problem. The child's rate of speech can also be calculated from the tape-recorded sample to identify whether this is having an effect on the child's fluency – or alternatively whether the level of stammering is adversely affecting the rate.

Is the child affected by the stammer?
This varies considerably; some children are not at all concerned by their stammering and will continue to communicate regardless of their difficulties while others become anxious and distressed by it. The therapist therefore spends time exploring the child's feelings and attitudes towards talking, and whether the stammer has any effect on his everyday life.

Note: It is our experience that encouraging a child to talk about the problem – not necessarily by labelling it – can be very helpful. It won't make it worse if handled sensitively and in a practical and constructive way.

How do the child's linguistic skills affect the stammering?
As described in Chapter 1, children who stammer may have other speech and language problems that may affect the development and maintenance of the stammer (Paden *et al.* 1999; Watkins *et al.* 1999).

Formal or informal assessments are used to evaluate the child's:

- understanding of spoken language;
- expressive language skills – use of grammar, vocabulary and word finding ability;
- development of speech sound skills;
- use of language such as asking questions, initiating conversation, responding appropriately etc.

In support of research findings, clinical experience also shows that some children who stammer may have quite subtle speech or language difficulties. There may be a 'word retrieval problem', which affects how efficiently they can select the right word from their 'vocabulary store'. It may be that they show uneven language skills, with good ability in one area, such as vocabulary, but deficits in another, for example, syntax. Therapy may need to focus on developing a child's linguistic skills as well as addressing the stammer.

Occasionally the assessments also reveal children with superior linguistic abilities. Parents sometimes describe their child as 'thinking faster than he can speak'. It has been suggested that these children are able to construct long complex language structures, but may not necessarily have the underlying speech motor skills required to express them fluently (Peters and Starkweather 1990).

Are the child's social communication skills affected?
It is estimated that by adulthood as much as 75 per cent of communication is non-verbal (Birdwhistell 1970). Over time, stammering can interfere with the appropriate use of eye contact, facial expression, listening, or turn taking: e.g. a child may look away or close his eyes as he attempts to say a difficult word, or find taking his turn more difficult when he is stammering. These will interfere with normal communication and therapy may need to include a social skills component (see Chapter 7).

The parent interview

This interview involves both parents (unless a single parent family). The aim is to obtain as complete a picture of the child within the family as possible, and also to engage both parents in the therapy process from the beginning.

It is worth repeating that parents often worry that they might have done something to cause their child's speech problem and it is therefore essential to reassure them that parents do not cause stammering. They are, however, the most knowledgeable people about their child and can provide information about the factors that may have contributed to the onset and development of the problem. They will also have a vital role in helping their child manage the stammer more successfully.

The interview questions are designed to tease out the factors that may be significant in determining a particular child's vulnerability to stammering and those that may be influencing its continuation.

The following four areas, based on research and clinical knowledge, may be covered during the interview and enable the therapist to formulate an hypothesis about the individual child's stammer.

Physical factors
- Family history of stammering.
- Family history of other speech/language/literacy problems.

- Other physical or coordination difficulties.
- Early developmental and health history, i.e. birth, milestones, hearing.

Linguistic factors
- The stammer: its onset, development, severity and variability and its impact on the family.
- Speech and language development.
- General communication skills.

Environmental factors
- Social and emotional factors that may be affecting fluency at home.
- Social and emotional factors that may affect the child's fluency at school.
- The linguistic environment, e.g. other languages, rapid speakers, sophisticated language models, turn taking.
- The response of others to the stammer.

Psychological factors
- The child's and the parents' anxiety about the stammer.
- Other emotional issues, e.g. family crises, bereavement.
- The child's personality.
- Other personalities in the household, sibling rivalry etc.
- Behaviour management, routines, consistency.
- The management of change and separation anxiety.

Assessment summary

The final stage of the assessment is to put all the information together from the child assessment and parental interview into a logical framework which attempts to account for the child's current stammer.

Time is spent sharing this summary with the parents so that they are able to understand why their child is vulnerable to stammering. This shared knowledge provides a basis from which the therapist and parents can work collaboratively to identify changes that are most likely to promote fluency.

Reports
Following the assessment a confidential clinical report is written which summarises the findings and makes recommendations for therapy as necessary. The report is usually sent to the parents in the first instance, for their comments and consent for distribution. It is then routinely copied to the child's GP and any other health professionals involved in his care, as requested by the parents.

Parents provide a copy of the report to the child's school or teacher at their own discretion. If a copy of the report is sent to the school by the speech and language therapist, it will usually be placed in the child's medical notes or SEN records.

Where there is a SLT service operating within the school the procedures for communicating information may be less formal. The therapist will be able to discuss the report with the parents and teachers, talk through the recommendations, and make action plans as appropriate.

Therapy

The type and amount of therapy available will vary but most specialists in the UK would agree that because stammering is not simply a 'speech' problem, recommendations for therapy could include:

- actively involving parents throughout;
- helping family members make small changes in the way they communicate with the child that may influence the stammer;
- working with schools to support and transfer skills learned in therapy;
- helping teachers and assistants identify any changes that might be beneficial;
- working directly on the speech fluency;
- addressing other speech and language problems;
- helping parents with the management of behaviour problems (if present);
- teaching more effective social communication skills.

Therapy for young children

Research has shown that early intervention is the most effective (Starkweather and Gottwald 1993; Curlee 1993; Onslow *et al.* 1994; Onslow and Packman 1999). The amount and type of therapy offered to a family will depend on the outcome of the assessment process, and may involve one or more of the following levels of care:

Information and advice
This would be recommended when:

- the parents are not anxious about the child's speech;
- the dysfluency is mild;
- the dysfluency is of recent origin;

- there is no history of stammering in the family;
- there are no concurrent speech and language problems;
- there are no other areas of concern.

Advice and guidance covering the following topics would normally be offered:

1. Information regarding the development of stammering.

2. The importance of family interaction styles including the influence of speech rates, rapid and/or frequent questioning, and the value of family rules for turn taking and listening.

3. Making opportunities for individual 'quality time' for the child with his parents.

4. Consistency within the household – that is, the influence of appropriate routines and reasonable boundaries for behaviour.

SEAN

Sean was three when his mother brought him to the clinic. The health visitor had suggested the referral, but since her older son had experienced a similar level of mild dysfluency she was optimistic about the outcome. There was no family history of stammering and Sean's speech and language skills were well within the norm for his age.

Although the speech had been quite hesitant for a few weeks she thought that it was 'on the mend'. The referral had been helpful in answering her questions, she felt more confident about managing the residual dysfluency. Sean was discharged at the review appointment three months later.

Indirect therapy
This would be recommended for parents who are concerned about their young child's speech, and while the dysfluency may still be variable there may be more evidence of tension and frustration. There could be additional 'vulnerability' in terms of a family history, or associated speech and language factors and aspects of family interaction styles that could be adjusted to promote the child's fluency.

In the early years the home environment has a significant influence on a child's developing communication skills. It is therefore the most appropriate place to help the child become more fluent.

Indirect therapy focuses on family interaction styles and is based on clinical and research evidence that changing even quite small aspects of the parents' communication style can have a real effect on helping their child to be more fluent (Rustin *et al.* 1996). Therapy in this case offers the parents the opportunity of looking at the ways they interact and communicate with their child and then helps them to identify some small changes that are likely to promote fluency.

Note: Parents do not cause stammering – but they have a really important role in helping the child become more fluent.

At the Oxford Dysfluency Conference in 1996, Nan Bernstein Ratner used asthma as a helpful analogy – parents do not cause asthma, but there are many ways in which they can manage the environment in order to reduce the impact of the problem.

Helping parents to make changes in the following areas can enhance the child's fluency and his confidence in communicating:

- matching the child's slower speech rate;
- increasing the pauses between exchanges;
- careful turn taking;
- reducing the length and complexity of sentences;
- engaging appropriate eye contact and adjusting other non-verbal behaviours;
- attentive listening;
- helping the child to lead play activities.

For further discussion see Nippold and Rudzinski 1995; Curlee and Siegal 1997; Guitar 1998.

Communication is a two way process; the way a parent (or anyone else) interacts will affect the child and vice versa. The features described above are closely linked, thus a change in one aspect will have an impact on another, which makes it difficult to identify which is the key to helping an individual to be more fluent. It is most likely to be a different combination for each child.

Parent Child Interaction Therapy
This is an indirect therapy programme used for this age group that is brief and effective (Rustin *et al.* 1996). The first phase consists of six one-hour hour weekly sessions and the second comprises a six-week consolidation period with a review and reassessment session at the end.

During the first phase a videotape recording is made of each parent playing with the child. The therapist then helps each parent identify aspects of their interaction style that they consider to be positive, and then some that they feel might be less helpful for the child's fluency. Discussing the pros and cons of particular changes is an essential part of the process – the parents are not being 'instructed', but are being given the opportunity to stand back and reflect on these issues. The therapy sessions are carefully structured to ensure that each parent only tackles one new target at a time, gradually building on the success of each step. They try out these changes with their child in the clinic and then at home, at first in time-limited, one-to-one, sessions. Gradually, those changes that are beneficial are incorporated into the interaction styles in the family.

> **EMMA**
> *In the first therapy session Mary, Emma's mother, noticed that she used lots of encouragement and eye contact when she was playing with Emma, and she felt that this was very positive, but she also observed that she was the one doing most of the talking! Mary decided to try to be less talkative during their play sessions – and see whether this helped Emma to say more. James, Emma's dad, observed that he looked as if he was really enjoying the play session – and so was Emma. However he also noticed that he was taking charge of the game – initiating, organising and instructing! James decided to try to be less organising as he anticipated that this would help Emma take the initiative more often and gain in confidence.*

As parents become more confident and relaxed about what they are doing and why, the child's experience of communicating changes and the dysfluency usually begins to decrease. By the end of six weeks parents often report that many aspects of their communication style have changed in ways that also benefit the other children in the household.

These gains are consolidated during the second six-week phase during which they do not attend the clinic but continue working towards the targets they have set themselves in the therapy sessions, maintaining regular contact by post and telephone. They return for a review and reassessment session during which the parents can provide information on progress, and the therapist can take measures of the child's fluency. Where progress is being maintained, the parents continue carrying out their targets at home, monitoring change, and returning 'homework' sheets. Further review appointments are made at three monthly intervals for up to one year (Matthews *et al.* 1997). The majority of families who have young children with this level of vulnerability to stammering will not need further intervention. There are a small number of children who may need further, more direct intervention to address residual fluency, language or phonological difficulties.

Indirect therapy plus direct therapy
This therapy recommendation would be for a child and the family where the stammering is causing a higher level of concern. Children who require this may be slightly older, with a longer history of stammering and other factors that are significant. Again there may be a family history, other speech and language problems and the child may be aware of and concerned about the problem.

Indirect: The Parent Child Interaction Therapy sessions would usually be the first phase, aimed at enhancing the interaction styles in the home environment. While these are likely to have a beneficial effect on the level of stammering, it may also be necessary to help the child to develop some strategies for managing the moments of stammering more successfully.

Direct: There are two components to stammering that need to be addressed in any therapy directed at modifying the problem – these are usually referred to as 'cognitive' and 'behavioural'.

The cognitive component of direct therapy aims to help the child understand three main concepts about 'stuttering and fluency':

1. *rate of speech*: for example, 'slow' versus 'fast' talking;

2. *disrupted speech*: for example, 'bumpy' versus 'smooth';

3. *tension and struggle:* for example 'hard' versus 'easy' talking.

The behavioural aspect of direct therapy uses modelling, imitation and positive reinforcement to help the child gain greater speech control. This could involve speaking more slowly, or finding an easier way to tackle the sounds that get 'stuck'. The methods used are adjusted for the age of the child and the therapist will use a carefully graded and structured programme of activities that gradually extend the child's ability to be fluent in a variety of circumstances.

Involving the parents continues to be important. They need to understand the process and participate in the sessions in order to help the child transfer new skills into his real world away from the clinic.

There are a number of commercially available treatment programmes that have been developed on the same principles. Many, including Parent Child Interaction Therapy, require additional training for therapists to feel confident in their use.

> **JOSH**
>
> *Josh and his parents completed a course of Parent Child Interaction Therapy, and both parents successfully made small but important changes in their communication styles when interacting with Josh. They demonstrated these changes within therapy and started to incorporate these skills into their everyday life. However, Josh continued to experience uncomfortable levels of stammering in certain situations. He was very aware of this, and explained how his words 'get jumbled up'. Direct therapy was introduced to encourage Josh to talk about his speech, and to help him experiment with ways to increase his fluency, such as slowing down his speech rate, and using 'easy starts' at the beginning of a sentence. Josh's parents continued to be involved in maintaining the changes they had made, and supporting Josh in the steps he was taking to increase his fluency.*

Direct therapy

Some therapists work directly on the speech as a primary intervention. The Lidcombe Programme (Onslow 1993), developed in Australia, has received considerable publicity and has published some encouraging results. Therapists using this programme should have been trained in its use according to the criteria established by its authors.

It is a behavioural programme conducted by the parent in the home and involves the systematic reinforcement of fluent speech with, in some cases, correction for dysfluencies. The

> **BEN**
>
> *Ben, aged four years, had a moderate stammer that was causing his parents considerable concern. He was very aware of his difficulties and when asked about his talking Ben was very 'matter-of-fact' and said that sometimes it was hard and at other times it was easy to talk.*
>
> *His parents were very anxious to help him and liked the idea of the Lidcombe Programme. They learned how to work with Ben on developing his awareness of his speech and encouraging him to use more of his fluent speech using positive reinforcement. Ben enjoyed being praised for his 'smooth' talking and liked playing games where he got stickers for speaking 'smoothly'. He was quick to pick up the idea of monitoring himself and was able to notice the words that were 'bumpy' and to repair them. As therapy progressed Ben became much more fluent, at first in carefully graded sessions and then increasingly in real life situations.*

parents are trained by a specialist therapist in the clinic to monitor their child's levels of fluency in different situations and then to carry out structured home practice sessions with a built in reward system.

The results of this programme demonstrate just how successful some children can be in learning to manage their own speech.

Therapy for primary school children

The age of the child and the length of time since the stammering started are always important factors in designing a therapy programme. The younger primary school child may well benefit most from the therapy described in the previous section. This section will consider the needs of children whose difficulties are more firmly established and less likely to resolve without help.

The child's level of awareness about his stammering may be influenced by the reactions of peers and others within his social environment. This may affect his confidence and self-esteem, and the stammering may become more noticeable as the child tries harder to mask it, or overcome it.

Therapy is directed at the child but with the parents (preferably both) involved at every stage. Therapy may be conducted on an individual family basis with the child, parents and siblings, as appropriate, attending weekly. It can also be organised as a group therapy programme on an intensive basis over two weeks or indeed on a weekly basis.

Treatment approaches will vary but many of the themes described previously apply and may also include the following:

1. Developing the family's awareness and use of social communication skills in the home environment.

2. Developing the child's understanding of stammering, fluency and communication.

3. Graded steps for modifying the stammer and enhancing the fluency.

4. Problem solving (see Chapter 7).

5. Strategies for developing confidence (see Chapter 7).

6. Transferring the new skills from the therapy room into the home and the school environments.

Indirect therapy – involving the family

In many households the stammer may have had an impact on the communication styles within the family. For instance, taking turns may have become unbalanced, perhaps other children in the house are quicker verbally, or conversely the child who stammers may have been allowed to take more and longer turns than others *because* of the stammer.

Using similar methods to the Parent Child Interaction Therapy in the clinic, the parents participate in discussions and activities to gain an understanding of interpersonal communication skills in relation to the child who stammers. In addition to the verbal aspects like rates of speech, level of questioning and complexity of language, non-verbal skills may also be included such as eye contact, listening, turn taking, praise and reinforcement, problem solving, and negotiation skills (see Chapter 7). In this way, the family can help to provide a communication environment that facilitates and supports fluency.

Direct therapy – cognitive and behavioural components

Therapists may use a cognitive approach where there is an emphasis on helping the child to understand more about the nature of stammering and fluency. The different circumstances that can influence the stammer are explored, and the role that thoughts and feelings can have in maintaining the problem.

The behavioural aspects encourage the child to experiment with alternative ways of managing the stammer. Therapists may use a variety of approaches in order to find the one that best suits the needs of the individual. Broadly these fall into two categories. The first is commonly referred to as 'speak more fluently' and may involve teaching children a technique such as slow, smooth or prolonged speech in structured steps, graded in difficulty. These methods of speaking aim to replace stammering with more fluent speech. The second is referred to as 'stammer more fluently' and aims to help children to experiment with their stammering in order to find an easier and more controlled way to stammer that reduces their anxiety and increases their fluency.

The strategies may include identifying moments of stammering and modifying them, rate control, easier onsets to words, and reducing tension in the speech muscles. Graded steps and well-defined stages would be used to make sure that the child and family understand the aims and objectives. In some cases these two approaches are integrated to meet the needs of individual children.

Transferring skills

Transferring the skills learned in therapy into everyday environments is undoubtedly the most difficult part of the therapy process, and requires the support of the family and the school. The first step is to help the child gradually extend their experience of using the fluency strategies at home following a schedule of small, manageable steps.

The same principles apply to transferring fluency skills into the school environment. Engaging the help of teachers in supporting the small steps a child is trying to take in the school setting can make the difference between success and failure. It may ultimately involve tackling situations like answering the register, reading out loud in class, or responding to questions where feelings of anxiety and fear of ridicule can make the stammer worse. Working with the child and the teacher on a structured step-by-step approach can make a difficult situation much easier to manage (see Chapter 5).

MATTHEW

Matthew was 11 and had two older sisters. He had a stammer that could be very mild at times but had periods when it was severe and caused considerable anxiety. Furthermore, he felt it was always at its worst in school. Therapy was directed initially at helping the family become aware of the communication styles in the household. They worked on eye contact, listening, turn taking, praise and reinforcement using video recordings of exercises for feed back and discussion (see Chapter 7 for exercises). The family also learned how to use a problem solving approach (Chapter 7) to resolve issues at home such as how to get ready for school on time. At the end of these sessions Matthew was feeling much better about himself and his speech had become increasingly fluent. However, it was clear that he wanted to feel more in control of his speech, especially at school. Sessions were arranged to work directly on his speech using both cognitive and behavioural strategies. He worked on slowing his rate of speech and making better use of pauses, but it was when he began to understand more about the way his worrying thoughts and panicky feelings were affecting his speech that things really started to improve at school (see Chapter 5). The final stage of therapy involved problem solving how he would like the school to help him. He decided that a meeting with his head of year and the therapist would give him an opportunity to explain his difficulties. Previously he had resisted all attempts by his parents to approach the school fearing that if they 'knew' he stammered it would somehow make it worse.

Therapy for pupils at secondary school

Stammering in teenagers and young adults is a complex, multidimensional problem which has at this stage usually become persistent or chronic. These individuals begin to develop strategies and avoidances as part of their stammering in an attempt to control, camouflage or conceal any appearance of being different. The self-concept of being a 'stammerer' with its elaborate web of negative beliefs may begin to dominate a young person's life.

At this stage of development, the peer group becomes increasingly influential. However, the parents continue to play an important part in supporting these pupils in the transition from childhood through adolescence and need to be included in the therapy process.

Individual and group therapy

The treatment that is offered might include individual or group therapy on a weekly or more intensive basis, while some will benefit from a combination of both. Individual sessions offer scope for a more 'tailor made package' directed at particular problems, while group therapy offers broader insights into the stammering and opportunities for sharing ideas and practising new skills in a safe environment.

The principles of therapy with this age group are very similar to those for the older primary school child, but here the focus is much more on the individual rather than the family and the activities and exercises will be adjusted carefully.

Thus the aims of therapy, whether on an individual or a group basis, may include the following:

1. To increase understanding of the nature of stammering and its development and to develop strategies for managing the stammering more successfully.

2. To improve social competence through communication skills training.

3. To explore the cognitive components of stammering, e.g. the role of negative thoughts and feelings, confidence and self-esteem.

4. To transfer and maintain the newly acquired skills.

The practical components to achieve these objectives could incorporate fluency control strategies, social communication skills, relaxation, problem solving and negotiation skills training (Rustin *et al.* 1995).

Understanding and managing stammering
The therapy clinic provides a supportive environment in which students can explore issues related to their stammering and experiment with various fluency strategies similar to those previously discussed. Learning to manage the stammer is a very demanding task. The aim is to help the individual to understand his particular stammering characteristics, identify the different skills involved in speaking, and experiment with various fluency strategies. These are then practised and tested out in situations graded by difficulty, e.g. home, school and socially. The overall aim will be to gain more voluntary control over a speech system which felt unpredictable and out of control.

Social communication skills
The skills of observation, eye contact, listening, turn taking, praise and reinforcement, problem solving, and negotiation are particularly important to this age group. Therapy that involves a group is ideal, as members of a well-gelled group will support each other, offer greater creativity, new ideas and provide opportunities to practise, making the process of learning and changing more enjoyable. The use of activities, exercises and brainstorms encourages the students to provide their own ideas and take personal responsibility for progress in therapy.

Cognitive components – confidence and self-esteem
Students are helped and encouraged to identify the negative thoughts and feelings that often have such a significant role in generating and maintaining the anxiety and fear associated with stammering. Therapy helps them to challenge this way of thinking and find other more helpful ways of approaching the problems they face.

Confidence and self-esteem are concepts that are often identified by students, parents and teachers as being at the core of the stammering problem. There is no doubt that lack of self-confidence in communicative situations is strongly linked with stammering.

Confidence and self-esteem can be developed in many ways but need reinforcement in order to be maintained.

There are two sources of reinforcement:

1. Through praise and encouragement from others such as parents, teachers and peers.
2. Self-reinforcement – being able to give oneself a 'pat on the back' and mean it.

Students need to discover ways of appreciating and applauding their strengths and achievements rather than 'putting themselves down'. An important part of therapy is helping students to identify how confidence is built and to practise self-reinforcement that is appropriate, honest and genuine.

JOE

Joe was 16 and very anxious about his oral exams. He had had therapy in the past and had a good idea about how he could modify his stammer in some controlled situations. He could be very fluent in therapy sessions and at times when he felt very relaxed. However, at other times Joe became very anxious and felt completely unable to control his speech. In therapy sessions he was able to identify the way his thinking affected his confidence, and that in turn had a direct influence on his ability to manage his speech. Joe was then in a position to challenge the way he was handling the difficult situations in an entirely new way, based around setting himself realistic and achievable targets. He also learned how to reinforce himself for his successes. Joe worked steadily over ten sessions towards his oral exam and was finally able to report that while he had not been fluent, he had managed his speech to his satisfaction and the stammer had not affected his examination. He passed with a good grade.

Transferring skills

It is a relatively straightforward task to learn new skills in a 'safe' and supportive environment, but these skills need to be transferred into the real world.

While it is important that the students develop their own graded targets, the role of the therapist is to ensure that the steps towards them are achievable and manageable and, where possible, also supported by the school and at home.

Summary of key points

- Speech and language therapists are responsible for carrying out detailed assessments of children who stammer.
- Assessments include fluency, language, and speech.
- Parents take part in the assessment and therapy process.
- It is important for all concerned to have a shared understanding of the problem.
- An action plan for therapy is developed to meet the needs of each individual.
- The type and outcomes of therapy differ with the age of the child.

- There is a focus on the development of social communication skills as well as management of the stammering for all age groups
- The type of therapy services available for children who stammer varies considerably throughout the NHS.

Therapy for preschool children
- Information and advice
- Indirect therapy
  e.g. Parent Child Interaction Therapy
- Indirect therapy plus direct therapy
    cognitive components
    behavioural components
- Direct therapy
  e.g. Lidcombe Programme

Therapy for primary school children
- Indirect therapy
  e.g. Parent Child Interaction Therapy
- Direct therapy
    cognitive components
    behavioural components
- Transferring skills learned in therapy to 'everyday' environments
- Individual or group therapy

Therapy for pupils at secondary school
- Group and individual therapy approaches
- Understanding and managing stammering
- Social communication skills
- Cognitive components
- Transferring skills

Figure 2.1 Therapy flowchart

Chapter 3

An educational perspective

Children who stammer, like all children, gain their seminal experiences over the many years they spend within the school system. It is here that they should develop the social, emotional and academic resources that they will need as adults but there are some children who need additional support in order to realise their potential.

Introduction

JOHN

John, now 27, vividly describes the moment when he realised he was different. He was 12 and, for many years, had successfully hidden his stammer at school until one day when he was asked to read aloud he found himself completely stuck on a word and then on what seemed like every word after that. The whole class looked at him, silent at first, then the laughter started. Thirteen years later the memory remains devastatingly clear. It was no-one's fault. It was totally unexpected, but it shaped John's life and colours his view of himself to this day.

Many adults describe similar painful memories from their schooldays:

- 'Just trying to say my name was a nightmare.'
- 'I couldn't say "Here, Sir" for the register.'
- 'Oral French was terrifying.'
- 'My panic rose as my turn to read came relentlessly closer.'
- 'If only someone had understood my problem.'

Speech and language therapists are often viewed as a source of support and guidance for young people who stammer and, as described in the previous chapter, there are many ways that speech and language therapy can and does contribute to an individual's ability to cope with the problem – but this may be limited by the confines of the health system and the lack of opportunity for cooperation between health and education. However, this chapter will examine the significant role that educational professionals can play in helping these children in school. It will discuss developments and recommendations regarding children with communication impairments and the demands of the curriculum at different stages, and it will highlight some classroom practices which can have a significant impact on stammering.

The focus of this chapter has necessarily been on England and Wales because these contain the largest proportion of school pupils. It is, however, recognised that Northern Ireland and Scotland have alternative systems for balancing their delivery of the curriculum and in terms of assessment systems. However, it seems that across the country, oral communication skills are being increasingly emphasised which will have implications for all students with any level of impaired communication.

Children with communication problems

The Green Paper *Excellence for All Children* (DfEE 1997) highlighted the longstanding difficulty in obtaining therapy services for school aged children with Special Educational Needs (SEN). There were many reasons for this, but it was clearly associated with the different statutory responsibilities and priorities between Local Education Authorities and Health Authorities – *politics and resources*. Although this applied to all therapy services, it was most apparent in speech and language therapy (SLT) for children with communication impairments. All parties agreed that there was a serious problem, but there was considerable and continuing debate about its resolution.

In November 1998, against this background of widespread concern, the Department for Education and Employment (DfEE), in partnership with the Department of Health (DH), established a working group to deliberate and reflect on the significant difficulties encountered in making appropriate speech and language therapy provision for children with SEN. The recommendations were published in November 2000 in a document entitled *Provision of Speech and Language Therapy Services to Children with Special Education Needs (England): Report of the Working Group*.

This document is important in relation to all children with significant communication problems, whether or not they have a statement of special educational needs.

The working party agreed that SLT provision should be based on a number of principles including that *nearly all children with communication problems have an educational need*, and that this need will be best met through *collaboration between parents, education and health within the educational context using models of best practice.*

The working party, stressing the need for collaboration, suggested that:

- Therapy is best carried out collaboratively within the school context.
- Assessment, diagnosis and therapy should be carried out in conjunction with teachers, parents/carers.
- Therapists should provide active support to help teachers differentiate content, teaching style and curriculum outcomes for children with speech and language difficulties.
- Therapists should provide education and training in relation to speech and language problems.
- A consultancy model can be used in some cases by speech and language therapists.

Partnerships between education, health and parents

The working group made thirteen final recommendations that included the following:

- Since communication is so fundamental to learning and progression, addressing speech and language impairment should normally be recorded as educational provision unless there are exceptional reasons for not doing so.
- The Government should consider expanding the drive on literacy to embrace a National Speaking Strategy for Schools, building on and enhancing speaking and listening aspects of the curriculum, together with a focus on pupils aged three and four and provision for targets.

The proposed National Speaking Strategy

And in relation to their proposed National Speaking Strategy they elaborate:

> The group believes that language comes before literacy. Pupils can only progress in their academic studies if they are confident that they can communicate with those around them. Failure to communicate – more particularly a failure on the part of others to appreciate the nature and extent of a child's communication difficulties – can lead to a sense of frustration and low self-esteem. It can undermine the child's confidence in his or her dealings with teachers and other pupils and can lead to isolation. It can also cause deep unhappiness. All of these may find expression in behavioural problems. (p. 13)

The group emphasised that a National Speaking Strategy would aim to:

- reinforce the importance of oral language;
- encourage a greater understanding of the nature of communication;
- facilitate early identification of communication difficulties and appropriate intervention; and
- promote greater collaborative working between education, health, parents and other agencies as appropriate.

But how does this apply to a child who stammers?

It is quite clear that the government's policy towards inclusion has increased the numbers of children with special educational needs in mainstream schools. This has placed many new responsibilities and demands on head teachers, teachers, Special Educational Needs Coordinators (SENCOs) and learning support assistants in terms of resources, curriculum delivery and time management. Children with statements of SEN can present with a wide range of complex or severe problems that often require additional specialist knowledge, training and skill in order to ensure their individual curriculum needs can be fulfilled as far as possible.

It is highly unusual for a child who stammers to have a statement of special educational needs but they may be on the register of special educational needs. *There is no doubt that stammering is a complex communication problem that can be affected, for better or worse, by a child's experiences within school.*

Why is stammering an educational need?

It seems to be relatively uncommon for teachers to come across a pupil who stammers in their classroom, although research indicates that about five per cent of young children go through a phase of dysfluency and one per cent of adults have a persistent stammering problem. One explanation that has been offered, but not researched, is that these children may be the 'quiet' ones who actively try to hide their stammering.

However, the increasing emphasis on oral skills of the past few years has generated many more enquiries from teachers and parents to organisations such as the British Stammering Association and The Michael Palin Centre for Stammering Children, asking how to help a stammering child in the classroom. The concerns raised are often about psychosocial issues like teasing and bullying, but also about helping the child deal with oral aspects of the curriculum. Teachers are often worried about whether certain class activities will make the stammer worse. They seek advice as to whether to include or exclude the child and how this might affect the child's confidence and willingness to participate: 'What should I expect of this child?' 'What can I do to help him when he stammers?' 'Are there particular strategies that will make it easier?'

Parents raise similar queries with regard to oral issues in the curriculum and, in addition, worry about more practical aspects like the child being fearful about asking to go to the toilet, or buying a meal in the school canteen, and, perhaps most importantly, their anxiety about teasing and bullying (Chapters 4, 5, and 6 discuss these particular points in more depth).

The initiatives to highlight oral skills, possibly with new targets for their acquisition, have implications for all children with communication problems but are also likely to bring to light many more children who stammer.

The quandary

Most children who stammer want to be 'the same': they want to participate and they want to be included. They often feel that they have something to contribute, that their ideas are equally good and that they should be given more opportunity.

However, these high expectations may not be matched by their behaviour. They can appear reticent, they may not contribute much in class or ask questions, they opt out and sometimes have letters from home asking for them to be excused from activities.

It is a dilemma for the child and inevitably difficult for the teacher to 'mind read' or understand what is happening for an individual child.

The teacher's role

In view of the lack of research evidence for effective curriculum and classroom management strategies for the child who stammers, it is only possible to provide recommendations on what is considered to be helpful practice (see also Lees 1999; Lees 2000; Stewart and Turnbull 1995; British Stammering Association). However, increased understanding about a disorder of communication, such as stammering, can make a vital difference to a student's personal and educational growth. Knowledge of the idiosyncratic nature of stammering and individual discussion and negotiation with the pupil offers the best possible prospect for helping him achieve educational success according to his ability and not limited by the stammer. As appropriate, the parent or carer should (according to the

Code of Practice) be involved in this too, depending on the age and wishes of the pupil.

Speaking and listening

As discussed, the National Curriculum was revised in 2000 and while the main *speaking and listening* activities are still based in the English curriculum for Key Stages 1–4, in attainment target one, a perusal of the whole National Curriculum framework demonstrates that there is a significant emphasis on oral communication across all subject areas. Additionally, there are now non-statutory guidelines for Personal, Social and Health Education which focus extensively on pupils' ability to take part in discussions, debates and other quite sophisticated oral activities.

The oral curriculum requirements for children who stammer are now very demanding and difficulties arise because teachers are simply directed to teach appropriate oral skills at all key stages in English, and to integrate them with the other two attainment targets in reading and writing.

For example, Key Stages for speaking and listening:

- KS1:   learn to speak clearly, thinking about the needs of the listener;
- KS2:   able to speak audibly and clearly in a formal context;
- KS3 and 4: able to speak fluently and appropriately in different contexts.

There is no explanation of the exact meaning of these terms for the teacher who is endeavouring to assess the pupil's speech within the criteria provided at the different levels.

The terminology is often imprecise and vague particularly in relation to children who stammer, for example – *clear speech, fluency or articulate speech*. Teachers are given no advice and left to their own perceptions. Consequently, while it would be useful to have more specific national guidelines, perhaps in the meantime it would be practical for the teaching staff to decide together on some working definitions for these terms, so that some consistent practice could be followed throughout the school in assessing the oral work of a pupil.

Communication skills for pupils and teachers

A greater emphasis on *communication skills* rather than speech fluency would also accommodate the needs of many children with speech problems. The speaking and listening targets do refer to these indirectly by stressing the need for children to take turns in speaking, and listen to others' points of view (KS2) and, later, the need to develop the skills of using gesture, tone, pace and rhetorical devices for emphasis (Key Stages 3 and 4).

For older students, teachers are now required to assess communication as one of the key skills across a range of subject areas. Students are expected more frequently to show evidence of their developing communication skills, for example by giving oral presentations or participating in and organising debates. It may be helpful for the primary and lower secondary teachers to look at the requirements for Key Stage 4 and the GCSE and A level syllabus (or equivalent in Scotland) to see what standards need to be eventually achieved.

It has been suggested that communication skills could be taught as a discrete subject, in the same way that some schools approach study skills so that these can be transferred across the curriculum. PSHE is an obvious vehicle for the delivery of such a course, and a partnership between teachers and SLTs could be very productive.

Joint communication skills training for teachers and SLTs

The recent working party on the provision of speech and language therapy referred to the need for teachers to gain more understanding of communication strategies (DH/DfEE 2000), and suggestions were put forward about providing continuous professional development jointly with speech and language therapists. DfEE funding is being made available to education authorities to encourage this.

Classroom practices which may impact on stammering

These are also discussed in Chapters 4, 5, and 6 in more specific terms. However, it is clear that there are certain situations that create higher levels of anxiety for these pupils. These may also be sources of difficulty to other students with communication problems.

Registration

Situations such as registration could be adapted to prevent the anxiety that children who stammer often associate with the requirement for quick responses in front of the whole class.

There are electronic registration systems available which avoid the need for a response but simple methods, such as raising a hand or noting the presence of children where the teacher knows them all, can also work effectively. The use of desk plans or name cards on desks have been used to help new and/or supply teachers.

If the child is identified as having a special educational need, then their individual education plan will contain strategies for dealing with the specific difficulties. However, as has been noted, many children who stammer will not be identified and these problems may only emerge over time. Where possible, sparing an individual child's anxiety in these routine matters would be very beneficial.

Reading aloud in the classroom

Some children, despite their stammering are quite confident about reading aloud in front of others, while for others this can be particularly difficult. There are no hard and fast rules for managing this situation that are helpful for all children, but there are some guidelines that may be useful.

When the stammer is clearly causing distress, some pupils might benefit from strategies such as:

- discussing options for reading aloud individually with the pupil, as an important first step;
- being given the reading material in advance;
- being offered choices as to when he will read;
- shared reading, across different subjects and classes;
- shared reading with different partners and in small groups;
- enlarging the group as confidence increases;
- reducing the time pressures, e.g 'amount' of reading rather than 'time constraints'.

The development of oral participation and confidence will not be linear. The child's attitude to the stammer will vary and, at each stage, new strategies may be needed or old ones revisited at different times.

Discussions/debates

These may take many forms and can include group work, paired work or whole class interactions where the teacher leads on a topic and pupils contribute. The variety of these will depend on the teacher and, to some extent, the needs of the subject, so it is unhelpful to be prescriptive. However, pupils are expected to make an oral contribution and to talk in front of a number of children, possibly in front of the teacher, or even in front of the whole class led by the teacher. In these situations, the degree of stammering may be more related to the individual's own beliefs and perceptions about the audience's reactions to their stammer, positive or negative, rather than the degree of difficulty of the task.

Most, but not all teachers will be operating within the ground rules already laid down within the classroom for oral work, and these need to stress that pupils should take their turns with speaking, listen attentively to others, follow the discussion carefully and make a contribution which builds on the comments of other speakers. In technical subjects the teacher will expect an understanding of the 'jargon' and will want to hear it correctly pronounced. These skills may be more difficult for children who stammer as their social use of language may not have developed to the level of some other children in the class and it is important that the teacher regularly reinforces the class code for the oral activities. The advantage of having a whole school policy for this, as discussed above, is that all staff will be operating in the same way and the pupil understands what the expectations are in every situation. The reaction of other pupils to all children who are speaking must be supportive and time spent discussing this is useful.

Group work

Teacher-led group work is illustrated in the guided reading activities of the Literacy Strategy and various forms of this will be found in any classroom. Good practice means that strategies will be in place for group organisation, e.g. a clear task and rules for interaction within the group clearly laid down.

The selection of group members needs thoughtful consideration about the needs of the children in the group and, if possible, should try to ensure that the children complement each other's abilities. The child who stammers may find it easier to be given a role in the group which has some significance but does not necessarily involve as much speaking as other roles. Perhaps he might act as recorder of the information, for example, which does involve close listening but would allow for slightly less oral participation. The pupil would feel that he was making a contribution and may, as a consequence, choose to join in the talking as much as the more fluent children.

Profiles for oral work

A developmental approach to the oral work, which provides differential opportunities as the child progresses through the whole of the educational continuum, is very useful, and it is possible for an oral profile to be built up throughout the school career. Some English teachers do this already and, when the information is collated and passed on to the next teacher, the targets achieved can be evaluated and others set. Such a coherent approach to the planning and setting of oral targets is supported by the National Curriculum in English and gives the pupil the opportunity to receive feedback for further development.

The school climate and oral communication

All schools now monitor their written communications carefully and may have developed sophisticated strategies. However, sometimes the equally important oral communication from the school does not receive the same attention. There is a case for developing a whole-school policy on speaking and listening and linking it with behaviour. There are schools which have devised a language and behaviour policy and the advantages of doing this are that the whole of the school community, the teachers, the ancillary staff, the governors, the parents and the pupils, could be involved in this debate.

Summary The increasing emphasis on oral communication skills in the National Curriculum is a double-edged sword for the children who stammer. On one side, it will mean that they may feel exposed by the demands of the system, but on the other that the needs of these children will be increasingly recognised. Strategies which support all children who are less skilled orally could be used to make a real difference to a child's confidence, and therefore to the degree of stammering.

There will be continued debate about whether a stammer constitutes a special educational need, but it is clear that when a problem is not identified formally it is less likely to be addressed by those specific strategies and targets which could change the child's life.

Chapter 4

The early years

Stammering tends to emerge in the nursery years: it is usually reported as starting between two and five years of age (Yairi *et al*. 1992). However, at this age many children are highly non-fluent as they attempt to organise their thoughts into language while they search for the right pronunciation, vocabulary, and grammar. Their speech may be hesitant and repetitive and yet full of urgency as they try to express themselves.

Introduction

Most children pass through this normal stage but some children go on to develop a stammering problem, and it is often during these early years that the first concerns may be raised, either by the child's parents or nursery staff.

This chapter is aimed at helping staff who work with dysfluent children in early years establishments and nurseries. There are suggestions for concrete ways of deciding whether a child might be vulnerable to stammering and, if so, practical ways of helping. Checklists and charts are included to help early years staff understand the child's difficulty. Suggestions are given for working together with parents and for making a referral to a speech and language therapist. Practical guidelines are presented for managing the child's problem within the early years setting.

The term 'dysfluency' will be used to describe the range of hesitant, repetitive and sometimes tense speech characteristics which may in later years become a stammering problem.

In general, concern about a child's fluency will be raised either by the parent or by a member of the early years staff. The following flowchart suggests the possible action that could be taken.

Identifying a problem

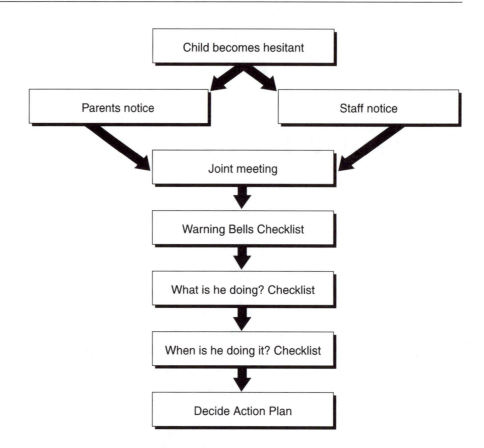

Figure 4.1   Flowchart for action

Parents notice the dysfluency

Parents who have noticed that their child has become dysfluent at home will probably want to establish whether the same thing is happening in the early years setting. They may also be seeking advice regarding what should be done.

Nursery staff notice the dysfluency

A member of staff may become aware of a child's increasing dysfluency, and feel unsure what to do about it. It may be helpful to ask other staff if they have noticed the child's dysfluency.

Joint meeting with parents and staff

If the child is being dysfluent in the early years setting, he is probably doing the same at home, but it may be less marked. Bringing the subject up with the parents can be a delicate task as causing undue alarm would be unfortunate.

The most appropriate approach might be an informal conversation during which the parents are asked how they feel their child is getting on in the nursery. If the parents do not raise the issue of the child's fluency it may be helpful to ask specifically about how they feel he is getting on with his speech. It is possible that well-meaning relatives, friends and professionals will have already advised them that they should not worry, as the child will grow out of the difficulty. However, it is very important to remember that, statistically, there is a chance that a child will outgrow the problem, but it would be unwise to tell every parent that their child is going to be fine as one in five children will continue to stammer into adulthood.

It may be necessary to mention to the parents that staff have noticed that the child's speech is sometimes hesitant in the nursery. The parents and early years staff might then agree to observe the dysfluency in both settings and then meet again to discuss what should be done.

If, at the next meeting, the parents and staff agree that there is some level of concern, the following checklist could be discussed and a decision can be taken together regarding any necessary action to be taken.

The Warning Bells checklist

Certain factors have been identified which give some indication about which children are more vulnerable, as shown in Figure 4.2. These are not indicators that the child will definitely stammer but they are warning signs that precautionary measures should be taken

1. If the answer to question 1 on the checklist is 'Yes' this indicates that the child may have inherited a predis-

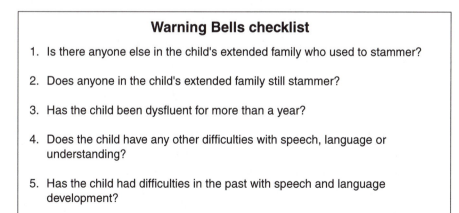

Warning Bells checklist

1. Is there anyone else in the child's extended family who used to stammer?

2. Does anyone in the child's extended family still stammer?

3. Has the child been dysfluent for more than a year?

4. Does the child have any other difficulties with speech, language or understanding?

5. Has the child had difficulties in the past with speech and language development?

Figure 4.2   List of vulnerability factors (see also p. 113)

position to stammer, but he may also have inherited the likelihood of overcoming the problem.

2. If a member of the child's extended family is still stammering, the child may have inherited this tendency.

3. If the problem has persisted for more than a year, it is less likely to disappear spontaneously.

4. If the child has any difficulties with speech sound production, spoken language, or understanding verbal language, he is more vulnerable to developing a stammer.

5. If, when the child was younger, he had problems with his speech or language development, he is more susceptible to a long-term stammering problem.

If any of the answers to questions 2, 3 4 or 5 are 'Yes' the child is more likely to develop a stammering problem, and a referral should be made to a speech and language therapist.

CHARLIE

Charlie was two years eight months when he started to repeat and prolong sounds. His words were also unclear and only his mother understood him most of the time

She was very worried because Charlie's father stammered when he was nervous, and as a child had been teased badly. It was clearly important that Charlie be referred to a speech and language therapist because of his vulnerability to stammering.

Characteristics of dysfluency

As discussed in Chapter 1, dysfluency can take many forms and can range from a mild repetitive behaviour to a tense, forceful struggle to speak. It is helpful to determine what the child is doing so that the level and variability of the problem can be monitored (Figure 4.3).

- *Revisions, interjections, phrase repetitions*: These speech behaviours are forms of hesitancy which are found in everybody's speech.
- *Repetitions*: These are also common to most speakers; however, most 'fluent' speakers tend to repeat a word or a syllable only once or twice, e.g. 'I hope she she hasn't forgotten.' Dysfluent children may repeat the word or sound up to eight times or more and this gives an indication of a greater difficulty.

What is he doing?

Is this child just hesitant or is he stammering?

Revisions e.g. 'I want a ...... some juice.' ☐

Interjections e.g. 'Can I um go outside?' ☐

Phrase repetitions e.g. 'My dog is ..... my dog is called Sam' ☐

Repeating the whole word e.g. 'But-but-but' ☐

   How many times? ☐

Repeating the first sound of the word e.g. 'C-c-c-can I?' ☐

   How many repetitions? ☐

Prolonging sounds e.g. 'Wiiiiill we ....?' ☐

Blocking sounds (mouth in position to speak but no sounds come out) ☐

Facial tension   eyes ☐   mouth ☐   other ☐

Body movements   hands ☐   feet ☐   other ☐

Disrupted breathing e.g. Gasping, speaking on incoming breath ☐

Child shows awareness

   Child says 'I can't say it' ☐

   Child gives up trying to say it ☐

   Child looks away during struggle to say it ☐

   Your instinct says child is aware ☐

   Child changes the word ☐

Figure 4.3 Monitoring the levelof the problem (see also p. 114)

- *Prolongations*: This can happen on either vowels, e.g. 'caaaan', or consonants, e.g. 'shhhhhe', and is a more obvious form of dysfluency.
- *Blocking*: This is a more severe form of dysfluency whereby the speech sound appears to get 'stuck', for example, 'I', the mouth is open but nothing comes out. Sometimes blocking happens at the back of the tongue, e.g. when saying the /k/ sound, or at the lips for a /b/ or /p/ sound.
- *Struggle or tension*: Struggle and tension in the breathing, face and body are also significant forms of dysfluency. The

child may gasp for breath, talk on an incoming breath, screw up his eyes, open his mouth very wide, grimace, cover his mouth, clench his fists, slap his thighs, or stamp his feet – all are signs that the child is trying to force the word out.

- *Awareness*: It can be difficult to ascertain if a young child is aware of his dysfluency. Sometimes the child seems to be conscious that something is wrong, but does not say anything about it, and people around may be fearful of bringing it out into the open. Another child may indicate his awareness verbally by saying 'I can't say the word,' or 'It's stuck,' or he may give up on his attempts to say a word. Sometimes a child shows awareness in his eyes when he is struggling to speak – he may briefly look away or there may be a flicker of discomfort in the eyes. Children sometimes change the word they are stuck on, e.g. 'Can I play with the saaaaa (sand) – the lego?' Parents and nursery staff may have an instinct that the child is aware of the dysfluency, based on nothing concrete, but nonetheless probably accurate. Although it is often assumed that young children are not aware of their dysfluent speech, Ambrose and Yairi (1994) demonstrated that children of approximately four years showed awareness. Clinical experience offers many examples of even younger children being aware of the problem: Craig, aged three years and two months, said to his mother 'I can't talk properly – my mouth is stuck'.

If the completed chart has more ticks towards the bottom of the page, the child's dysfluency is a cause for concern. If this combines with any of the 'Warning Bells' from the list of vulnerability factors, then the child's problem is less likely to get better without some kind of help. However, even if the dysfluency is a milder type (with most of the ticks at the top of the page) it is worth monitoring as the problem may persist or develop into a more severe form. Again, if this combines with any of the warning bells, it is important to be alert to the possibility of a stammering problem.

Variability of dysfluency in young children

Dysfluency is at its most variable in young children. There may be episodes of apparently 'severe' dysfluency but then long periods of fluency when the problem seems to have resolved, only to return suddenly. In addition to these fluctuations over long periods of time, the problem may also vary from day to day, from word to word and from one speaking situation to another. Parents frequently report that there seems to be no pattern to help them understand the problem.

It is not clear why dysfluency varies so much. Sometimes there are obvious links to the child's state, e.g. the dysfluency is worse because the child is overtired or ill or upset. But equally at another time the child may be ill or upset and his speech is fine.

Certain factors sometimes seem to account for the variation in a child's fluency on a daily basis:

- When the speaking task is too complicated, e.g. the child is trying to describe something that happened in the past.

Situation checklist

The child stammers when he is:

Talking to himself or his toys ☐

Talking to other children ☐

Shouting ☐

Singing ☐

Explaining something to an adult ☐

Answering a question in a one to one setting with an adult ☐

Answering a question in a group ☐

Competing with other children to say something ☐

Figure 4.4 Variability of dysfluency (see also p. 115)

This may make the child more dysfluent than if he were trying to describe a picture in front of him.

- When the speaking situation is more pressured, e.g. if a stranger asks the child for his name. However the same child might be able to give his name fluently when asked by another child.

Observing the child over a period of time may reveal certain patterns within the variations, for example he is always fluent when he is running around the playground and shouting, but he is nearly always dysfluent when he is trying to say something before another child interrupts. The checklist in Figure 4.4 will help to identify what is happening.

The action plan

When the checklists have been completed the nursery staff and the parents can decide on a plan of action together. This may be:

1. Immediate referral to a speech and language therapist. This is appropriate if the child is experiencing significant difficulties, and there are indications of vulnerability to a persistent problem or if there is considerable anxiety about the child's speech.

Or

2. If the dysfluency seems milder and there is less concern about the problem, then the child's progress could be monitored for six weeks or so, and if the problem is persisting or getting more obvious a referral can still be made.

Referring to a speech and language therapist

When there are any indications that a child might be vulnerable, early referral to a speech and language therapist is strongly recommended. See Chapter 2 for the referral procedure. It is preferable to make an early referral that turns out to be unnecessary rather than 'wait and see', as the child's difficulties may become more complicated and entrenched.

'Is he putting it on?'

The answer to this is probably not. Stammering hinders normal communication and few children would deliberately sabotage their means of expressing themselves and having their wishes granted.

'Is he copying another child who stammers?'

Children do copy one another but this tends to be very transient. Stammering is not 'catching' – it may be present in more than one family member but this is probably due to genetic and environmental factors (see Chapter 1 for more information). It is advisable to take a credulous approach to any child who is showing signs of dysfluency in order to give him the best chance of overcoming it.

'Did I do something to make him dysfluent?'

People cannot cause a child to become dysfluent. Parents often report that they fear they may have done something to make the child dysfluent, but research has shown that this is not the case. Similarly, nursery staff and teachers cannot cause dysfluency. Figure 4.5 summarises the most helpful responses to the dysfluency.

It's fine to be sympathetic

Generally, people do not need to be told how to deal with a child who is hurt or upset or struggling with a task. The instinctive reaction is to comfort, help and reassure the child. If the child is desperately trying to do up a button, an adult would usually praise his efforts, encourage him, console if it proves too difficult and offer assistance if appropriate. They would not ignore the child's difficulty.

The same principle applies to the way adults should react to a child who is struggling to get his words out. The natural response would be to commiserate, 'That was a hard word to say, wasn't it?'; to praise, 'Well done, you said it'; to comfort with a reassuring touch or word; or to offer help if the child gives up, 'Did you mean the sand or the play dough?'

There is often concern that acknowledging a child's difficulty might be drawing his attention to it and somehow creating a problem. But there

---

What you can do to help

- It's fine to be sympathetic

- Don't feel under pressure to say the word for him

- Ask the child what he would like you to do

- Help him to feel there's no hurry to finish
  - use more pausing
  - try to talk at the same speed as the child
  - watch your body language

- Help him to keep his language simple
  - keep your own language simple
  - use simple questions

- Encourage all the children to take turns

- Help the child develop in confidence

Figure 4.5 What staff can do to help the dysfluent child (see also p. 116)

is no evidence that this can happen and, on the contrary, children may feel under less pressure once they know that someone understands and their difficulty is brought out into the open.

Don't feel under pressure to say the word for the child

Watching children struggle with any task can be uncomfortable – there is a strong urge to help them put a piece in the form board or thread the bead on to the lace.

However, an adult's level of frustration and anxiety while watching a child strive to complete a task is probably different to that of the child. He may be blithely unaware of anybody else's discomfort, and happy to carry on until the task is finished.

Listening to a child who is blocking on every word can be upsetting and feelings of compassion, frustration, impatience and a sense of helplessness make us want to take over and end the child's distressing efforts to speak. It may be very obvious what the child is trying to say and there is a great temptation to say the word for the child.

However it is important to be aware that, while some children may be happy for people to finish off their words for them, many would prefer that the listener waited for them to get their words out.

Tip: A rule of thumb is to avoid finishing the child's words.

Ask the child what he would like you to do

There is no universally correct way of responding to a child when he is dysfluent but, with parental consent, and if it has been established that the child is aware of his difficulty, it may be helpful to consult the child about how he would like the situation handled, e.g. 'You know you said that sometimes your words get stuck when you are trying to talk. Well, is there anything you would like me to do when you are having trouble, or should I just listen and wait until you have finished?'

The child might have some ideas of how the adult could help, e.g. the adult showing that he is still listening, making sure the other children don't interrupt before he has finished. Alternatively, the adult could make some suggestions, e.g. 'Would it help if I put my hand on your arm to show you I'm listening and I can wait?'

Help the child to feel there is no hurry to finish speaking

Talking quickly gives a speaker less time to think, to plan what he is going to say, to choose the right words, put them into sentences and use the correct speech sounds so that he can be understood.

The most common response to a dysfluent child is to say 'Slow down', 'Take it easy', or 'Take your time'. The principle of this reaction is absolutely correct – slowing down would give the child more time and help him be more fluent.

However, it is extremely difficult to slow down our rate of talking, especially when we are excited, in a hurry, or competing with others to say something first. Adults find it very hard to slow themselves down – it requires patience, concentration and the ability to self-monitor. Preschool children find it impossible to follow the instruction to 'slow down'. The target of slowing the child down therefore needs to be approached differently.

Use more pausing

A useful way to create the impression that there is no hurry to speak is the use of pausing. Pausing to think before starting to talk gives the speaker time to organise his thoughts into words and the words into sentences etc. A young child who is in a phase of accelerated language acquisition would benefit especially from such space and time.

The adult can model this pausing, waiting a couple of seconds before replying to a child's question, or before moving on to the next topic. The pausing can be accompanied by a physical gesture to indicate that the teacher is thinking, e.g. a finger placed on the cheek, or a verbal filler like an 'um' or 'er'.

Tip: The notion of pausing to think, or 'thinking time', is a good topic to discuss with a whole group of children.

Slow down your own speech

If somebody speaks to us in a calm and unhurried way, we are more likely to reply in similar tones. Nursery staff can try to speak more slowly to the dysfluent child. If the adult is talking as slowly or even more slowly than the child, it can help the child be more fluent. However, it is best to start with short periods of slower talking as this can be hard to maintain for any length of time. It may be helpful to practise in a quieter environment, maybe in a one to one setting with another child, where there are few distractions or pressures to hurry up. Tape recording the rate of speech can give useful feedback, or asking a colleague to monitor the speed.

Tip: The most useful response when the child has difficulty talking is not to tell the child to slow down but to slow your own speaking rate.

Watch your body language

Even when an adult is talking slowly and using pausing, it is still possible that a sense of urgency or impatience exists. It is useful to consider, 'Is there anything about me that might be leading this child to think that he has to hurry up?' e.g. fidgeting, doing something else at the same time, repeatedly nodding.

Help him to keep his language simple

Dysfluency tends to occur on longer, more complex sentences. A child who is trying to construct a difficult sentence with high level vocabulary might stumble more than if the sentence has a simple structure with common, familiar words.

Young children are in a phase of accelerated learning of vocabulary and grammatical structures. It would not be desirable to hinder this learning, so it is important to strike a balance between encouraging the child's language development at his own pace, and removing extra demands upon his fluency.

If a child has language difficulties, an assessment by a speech and language therapist will help determine the appropriate level of language input. Once nursery staff have an understanding of a child's linguistic abilities, they can help that child not to overstretch his capacity to be fluent by setting the appropriate level in a conversation.

Keep your own language simple
The complexity of an adult's language will influence the linguistic level that a child attempts. It is easier for a very young child to talk in the 'here and now' about concrete things that are present, than it is to talk in the abstract about ideas or events in the past or future. A dysfluent child may be fluent when commenting during play, but then become dysfluent when trying to talk about a recent trip to the zoo. It is therefore helpful if the adult keeps to concrete topics whenever possible in a conversation with a dysfluent child.

The adult can also model the use of shorter sentences with common vocabulary, instead of talking in complex sentences with high-level vocabulary. For example:

Helpful model	'You've put the lion in the cage with the tiger. I hope they don't fight'
Less helpful model	'Lions and tigers should go in separate cages because they might turn on each other. Do you remember when we went to the zoo and we saw them in different surroundings.'

Tip: The shorter your sentences, the simpler your language.

Use simple questions

Answering a question can be one of the most demanding verbal tasks. There is pressure to think of a response, formulate the language, and express it clearly, all within the time constraints of the questioner's attention. If several people are competing to answer the question at the same time, the pressure is greater.

Different question forms pose varying levels of difficulty:

Easier	Yes/No questions	e.g. 'Do you need the toilet?'
	Forced alternatives	e.g. 'Would you like milk or water?'
	'What' questions	e.g. 'What is this?'
	'When' questions	e.g. 'When do you have a bath?'
	'Why/How' questions	e.g. 'Why do people brush their hair?'
		'How did you get here today?'
Harder	Open ended questions	e.g. 'Tell me about . . .'

Questions are an essential tool for communication and cannot be avoided completely when talking to a child. However, modifying the level and quantity of questioning so that it becomes less verbally demanding (and thereby less demanding of the child's fluency) may be helpful for a child who is dysfluent.

Tip: The shorter the child's answer, the easier it will be for him to be fluent.

Encourage children to take turns to talk

Turn taking is an integral and necessary feature of most early years settings. Nursery staff use a variety of strategies to teach young children the convention of waiting their turn to play, talk, jump on the trampoline etc.

Turn taking is an especially important issue for the dysfluent child. As previously discussed, factors which are likely to increase dysfluency are:

- trying to talk too quickly;
- competing with other children to say something.

When a group of children is asked a question, a number of them will try to be the first to respond. As one child is answering, the others will continue to indicate that they also have something to say. The first child is then under pressure to finish quickly before another child cuts him off. If this first child has a tendency to be dysfluent, it is highly likely to happen at this point, which delays his response further and increases the potential for interruption. If, on the other hand, the dysfluent child knows that others will listen and wait for him to finish speaking before they talk, then he will feel under less pressure to think and talk quickly.

The early years setting may be the first place a child encounters the need for turn taking. The widely used convention of raising hands to indicate that we want to talk is a very helpful, concrete practice in teaching children not to talk simultaneously or interrupt. However, even within a 'put up your hand' system, pressures may still exist for the dysfluent child, so it may be helpful to further develop the convention of turn taking. The rules of turn taking (Appendix 5) could be discussed with the whole class and further activities to develop children's turn-taking skills are suggested in Chapter 7.

It is important to reiterate that even if the speaker is the dysfluent child, people should not be afraid to tell the child at an appropriate juncture that he has had a long enough turn to talk and he should let somebody else have a turn.

Help the child develop in confidence

These children are not necessarily lacking in confidence or more nervous or anxious than others, but the ongoing experience of having difficulty talking can progressively undermine a child's self-esteem. It is therefore important to take steps to build a child's confidence about all aspects of himself. A child's self-esteem can be developed by becoming more aware of his strengths, e.g. 'I am helpful at tidy up time.' 'I am kind to other children when they are sad.' 'I am careful when I do colouring in.'

In Chapter 7 there are suggestions about ways that children's self-esteem can be built up using descriptive praise, rather than just saying 'Well done' or 'Good boy'. Praise that is specific and descriptive helps a child to develop a positive vocabulary about himself, which develops his self-esteem and confidence.

Tip: Supply the child with a positive vocabulary about himself.

Actions that may not be helpful for the dysfluent child

In their attempts to assist the dysfluent child people may, sometimes unwittingly, respond in an unhelpful way.

Avoid treating them differently

The suggestions made in this chapter can be applied to all children, whether they are dysfluent or not. Few nursery staff can devote themselves exclusively to one child and the principles can benefit the whole class, building social, listening and speaking skills in every child, as recommended in the Foundation Stage Curriculum.

Avoid talking for the child

It has been established that supplying the word that a child is having difficulty in saying is not generally advisable. Sometimes parents explain how they try to protect their children from having to be dysfluent by answering questions on their behalf, before the child has the chance to get into difficulty. Although obviously well meant, this may affect the child's view of himself as a communicator, and encourage him to opt out of potentially difficult speaking situations. It is therefore advisable not to pre-empt the child's response, but let the child speak for himself. It may also be necessary to stop other children from trying to speak for the dysfluent child.

Avoid asking the child to 'perform' verbally

Parents and other adults may unwittingly put a child under pressure when they tell the child to 'perform' verbally in front of others. This may be as simple as 'Tell the lady your name' or may be more complex, e.g. 'Tell Mummy that you need to bring in a pair of wellington boots tomorrow for our footprint picture.' Such assignments may be too demanding for the child and it would be preferable to give him a note to take home.

Use normal eye contact

Eye contact is a natural, unconscious aspect of communication. When communication is disrupted, it may be difficult to tell if it is appropriate to look at the speaker or not. There may be a sense that if the listener looks away, he is saving the speaker embarrassment. However, looking away might be interpreted as boredom, discomfort, or a desire to get away. Advice leaflets on stammering often advise the listener to maintain eye contact with the person who is stammering. However, there may be a tendency to go to the opposite extreme and stare unnaturally. Fixing the child with a wide-eyed stare gives the impression of urgency and tension, which is counterproductive. Aim to use normal and relaxed eye contact to show the child you are listening and have time to wait for him to finish.

Tip: Concentrate on *what* the child is saying and not *how* he is talking.

Avoid letting them monopolise the talking

Another piece of advice that is often given about stammering is 'Don't interrupt the child – make sure he is given time to finish.' When children are encouraged to take turns to talk and not interrupt one another, it is possible that the dysfluent child may start to talk at length, because he knows he holds the floor and will not be cut off. Adults may fear curtailing these long monologues because of the dysfluency, even though they would readily tell another child to stop and let somebody else have a turn. The outcome might be that the dysfluent child becomes used to being allowed to talk uninterrupted and doesn't learn how much talking is appropriate. The dysfluent child needs to learn to take his turn and end his turn after an appropriate time, and it may be necessary for the adult to break in with 'Thank you Emma, now let's hear what Joe has to say'

Dealing with difficult questions: 'Why does Sam talk like that?'

Young children tend not to have inhibitions about commenting on different characteristics in the people around them: 'Why have you got that lump on your face?'. When they notice the hesitant speech of the dysfluent child, curiosity prompts them to ask about it. This bears none of the malice which may characterise the cruel teasing the child may encounter in later years. It is appropriate therefore to respond to the question seriously and carefully: 'Sam is talking like that because it is sometimes hard for him to get the words out. He knows what he wants to say; he just needs more time to say it. So we can help him by waiting for him.'

What to expect of the speech and language therapist

Therapy with young children can be very effective, so early referral and intervention give the greatest cause for optimism. While treatment of stammering offers no guaranteed cure, it provides the parents and child with strategies for helping with the problem. For the young child who has only just begun to be dysfluent, these strategies may be sufficient to resolve the problem altogether. In some cases, the fluency improves but the dysfluency may return at a later time, possibly during a time of stress or excitement, e.g. illness, change of school, Christmas. If the problem persists into primary school years, the therapy will change, becoming more focused on the child managing the stammer with the support of his parents.

Chapter 3 gives a brief overview of speech and language therapy that might be offered to children at different ages.

Summary

During a child's early years he is highly likely to be hesitant as his speech and language skills mature. There are some factors which can indicate whether the child is vulnerable to this hesitancy becoming a long-term stammering problem. Early years staff can, together with the child's parents, decide whether it is appropriate to refer the child to a speech and language therapist. They can also help the child to become more confident about communicating in the early years setting, by trying some of the strategies suggested.

Chapter 5

The primary school child

Introduction

Many children are highly dysfluent in their early years, and for most this is a transient phase that will no longer be apparent when they start primary school. However, for some children the hesitations may persist and become increasingly tense, causing anxiety in the child, his parents and teaching staff.

This chapter will describe the range of stammering behaviour which may be found in a primary school child. Checklists are included to help identify the nature of the stammer and how the child's school life may be affected by it. Suggestions are given for managing parents' concerns about their child who stammers, as well as liaising with a speech and language therapist. Practical guidelines are given for helping the child in the classroom setting.

Identifying the problem

Stammering can take many different forms and every child who stammers will do so in his own unique style. It is therefore helpful to establish exactly what the child is doing so that the level of the problem can be monitored. The checklist provided (Figure 5.1) can be used to record the child's stammering behaviour in school, and this information will make a valuable contribution to a speech and language therapist's assessment.

Some very young children display tense symptoms of stammering with associated body movements like hand clenching and foot stamping. On the other hand, a child at Key Stage 2 may be repeating sounds or syllables without any evident struggle.

A primary school-aged child is likely to be aware that he has a stammer, even though he may not have a label for it, and he may also be unconcerned about it as awareness does not necessarily imply anxiety.

In many cases a child's stammering changes as he becomes increasingly self-conscious about his difficulty. He may develop his own tricks for getting the words out, e.g. by nodding his

---

Describing the stammer

Word repetitions	☐	**Sound or syllable repetitions**	☐
E.g. but but but		E.g. C-c-c-c-can I?	
Number of repetitions	☐	Number of repetitions	☐

Prolonging sounds	☐	**Blocking sounds**	☐
E.g. wiiiiiiil we		(mouth in position but no sound)	

Facial tension   **Body movements**

eyes	☐	head	☐
mouth	☐	hands	☐
other	☐	feet	☐
		other	☐

Disrupted breathing ☐
E.g. gasping, talking on incoming breath

Awareness   **Avoidance**

Says 'I can't say it'	☐	Changes words	☐
Gives up trying to say it	☐	Avoids words	☐
Looks away during struggle to say it	☐	Avoids situations	☐
Your instinct says he is aware	☐	Uses fillers	☐
		Concealing stammer	☐

Figure 5.1   Describing the stammer (see also p. 118)

head or finger tapping. He may try to avoid or disguise the problem by:

- *Changing words*: This type of avoidance may be obvious to the listener, as the child struggles to say a word then gives up and says the same thing using a different word, e.g. 'I'm ssss . . . I'm sssss . . . (starving) . . . I'm hungry.' Sometimes children may even completely change what they were going to say, e.g. 'Please can I have a bar of ch-ch-ch . . . (chocolate) . . . some smarties.'

- *Avoiding situations*: If the child experiences difficulty on a regular basis with talking in a certain context, he may decide to opt out altogether, so for example the child stops raising his hand in class even though he knows the answer to a question. Other situations a child may avoid in school are: participating in assemblies or drama productions, reading aloud in front of the class, or taking messages to another member of staff.

REECE

Reece, who was eight, said that he would ask to go to the toilet whenever there was an activity in class that he knew would be difficult for his speech.

- *Using fillers:* Natural conversational speaking is never totally fluent: pauses, repetitions, restarts and the use of fillers such as 'um' and 'er' are common, and not noticed by the listener. Children who stammer may adopt the use of other, less typical fillers as a strategy to help them get through a difficult word, which often leads to further confusion, e.g. 'My nn . . . well my nn . . . well my name is J-J-J well John.'
- *Concealing the stammer:* Children can become adept at hiding their difficulties, by using distraction tactics such as pretending not to hear the question, dropping books, or disguising the stammer by coughing or putting on a funny voice.

Variability of stammering

Stammering is at its most variable in the early years. Many children will experience periods of fluency that may last several days or weeks but then start again for no apparent reason. As they progress through primary school, the problem is more likely to become entrenched, but can still vary enormously from day to day or from one situation to another.

This level of unpredictability can often leave both the child and the adult feeling frustrated and anxious.

CHRISTOPHER

Jane reported that when her son Christopher was six, he was told off because an adult had heard him talking fluently to his friends at playtime, and stammering when she asked him a question. The child was told to 'stop putting on that stammering voice'.

A checklist (Figure 5.2) can be used to monitor the fluctuations in a child's stammering and note how this changes as he progresses through school. This information will also be useful to a speech and language therapist.

Why does it fluctuate?

The checklist will provide a record of how the stammer varies but not why. The reasons are not always obvious, but certain factors undoubtedly affect a child's fluency (Figure 5.3):

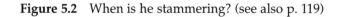

When is he stammering?	
When he is talking to himself	☐
When he shouts	☐
When he sings	☐
When he is talking to his class teacher	☐
explaining something	☐
answering a question	☐
competing with other children to answer	☐
other teachers and school staff, e.g. lunchtime assistants	☐
the head teacher	☐
When he is reading aloud	
in a one to one setting with the teacher	☐
in a small group setting	☐
in front of the class	☐
in front of the school (e.g. assembly)	☐
When he is talking to children informally	☐
When he is talking in a small group of children	☐
When he is talking in front of the class	☐
When he is talking in front of the school	☐
When he answers the register	☐
When he takes messages to other members of staff	☐
When he is being told off	☐
When he seems excited	☐

Figure 5.2 When is he stammering? (see also p. 119)

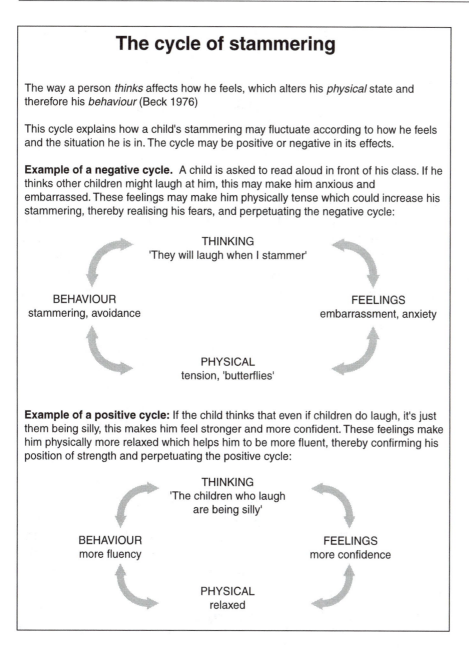

The cycle of stammering

The way a person *thinks* affects how he feels, which alters his *physical* state and therefore his *behaviour* (Beck 1976)

This cycle explains how a child's stammering may fluctuate according to how he feels and the situation he is in. The cycle may be positive or negative in its effects.

Example of a negative cycle. A child is asked to read aloud in front of his class. If he thinks other children might laugh at him, this may make him anxious and embarrassed. These feelings may make him physically tense which could increase his stammering, thereby realising his fears, and perpetuating the negative cycle:

THINKING
'They will laugh when I stammer'

BEHAVIOUR
stammering, avoidance

FEELINGS
embarrassment, anxiety

PHYSICAL
tension, 'butterflies'

Example of a positive cycle: If the child thinks that even if children do laugh, it's just them being silly, this makes him feel stronger and more confident. These feelings make him physically more relaxed which helps him to be more fluent, thereby confirming his position of strength and perpetuating the positive cycle:

THINKING
'The children who laugh
are being silly'

BEHAVIOUR
more fluency

FEELINGS
more confidence

PHYSICAL
relaxed

Figure 5.3   The interactions of thinking, feelings, physical state and behaviour (see also p. 120)

The language:	the child is more likely to stammer when he is attempting to explain something long and complicated.
The situation:	the child may be affected by having to talk to a stranger, having an audience, having to answer quickly before other children interrupt, or being reprimanded.
The thoughts:	the child's fluency will be affected by worrying thoughts and

The feelings: feelings of anxiety, excitement, embarrassment, etc.

The *language* and *situation* are likely to have a bigger impact on a child in Key Stage 1, whereas *thoughts* and *feelings* play a greater part as the child progresses through Key Stage 2.

Talking to the parents of the child who stammers

The onset of stammering is usually in the early years, so a child may start at primary school with an established difficulty.

Parents may be very anxious about their child's stammering, and may have sought advice and reassurance from several quarters. As previously discussed, research has shown that one in five children do not outgrow the problem, and that the longer the child has been stammering, the more complicated the stammer becomes, often with associated emotional, social and educational consequences.

It may therefore fall to the teacher to advise the parent that it would be appropriate to have the child referred for assessment by a speech and language therapist. For information on how to refer, see Chapter 2.

Some questions teachers may have

'Should I say the word for him?'

It can be difficult to wait for a child who is struggling to express himself, especially when there are so many other demands on a teacher's attention. It is tempting to supply the word for the child, thus putting him out of his misery and allowing the teacher to move on. However, it is not always possible to anticipate exactly what the child wants to say, and some children find it very frustrating to have the wrong word supplied. Moreover, clinical experience has demonstrated that many children who stammer would prefer that the adult waited for them to say the word, rather than fail in their attempt to finish the sentence.

Tip: Just listen and wait.

'Should I let others speak for him?'

Other children may attempt to help a child who stammers by speaking on his behalf, anticipating what he wants and saving him the struggle to say it. Although obviously well meant, this should be discouraged, and children should be advised to let the child speak for himself while others listen and wait.

'Should I tell him to take deep breaths?'

When a child is struggling to say a word, it may seem that he doesn't have enough breath in his lungs, and the natural response is to tell the child to take a deep breath. However, this can result in a build-up of tension around the chest, throat and mouth, thereby increasing the likelihood of stammering. It is counter-productive to tell a child who stammers to take a deep breath. Instead, most children prefer an adult to just listen and wait for them to say the word.

'Should I encourage him to try difficult speaking tasks?'

A rule of thumb is to encourage the child who stammers to attempt tasks that he is keen to try, but not to push him to do things that he feels are too difficult. It is therefore important in the first place to ask the child how he feels about the task. It should not be assumed that a child would not want to take part for fear of stammering, he may prefer to do it and stammer rather than be left out of the activity.

Assemblies and other performances
Children who stammer should be given the opportunity to choose whether they want to take part in performances. The role taken need not be mainly verbal; it could involve mime, dance or song. It is useful to remember that these children often find that they can speak fluently when they are acting, putting on an accent or role-playing the part of another person. Children who stammer are also usually fluent when they are talking in unison with others, so the child may be given a role with another child in which they read or recite together.

> **KOPAL**
> *Kopal, who was ten, had a severe stammer and had always avoided taking any verbal parts in school productions. Her teacher asked her to try out a small part of an American girl and, to her surprise, Kopal found that she could do so completely fluently. The part was then developed and Kopal revelled in her first experience of a leading role.*

Parents may express concern about their child performing and possibly stammering. Teachers may have to deal sensitively with this desire to protect their child from possible discomfort, especially when the child does not seem to share their fears!

Tip: If in doubt about what to do, ask the child.

'Where should I look?'

Some people find it difficult and embarrassing to witness a child struggling to talk, and may look away to spare the child's feelings. However, this break in eye contact may be interpreted by the child as a loss of interest or a desire to escape. Sometimes the listener may go to the other extreme and fix the child with an uncomfortable stare. It is most helpful when people maintain easy balanced eye contact, just as they would if the child was talking fluently.

Tip: Try to focus on what the child is trying to say, rather than how he is saying it.

What the teacher can do to help the child

1. Acknowledge the problem.
2. Be flexible with oral tasks.
3. Raise awareness among all school staff.
4. Help the child feel there is no hurry to finish speaking.
5. Help him not to be too ambitious in what he is trying to say.
6. Encourage the class to take turns.
7. Build the child's confidence.

Acknowledge the problem

If it is clear that the child is aware of the stammering problem (see 'Describing the Stammer' checklist in Appendix 6), then it will be appropriate for the teacher to acknowledge the child's difficulty, just as one would if a child was struggling to tie up his shoelaces. This acknowledgement may take the form of:

- a sympathetic comment: 'That was a bit of a struggle, wasn't it?'
- an observation: ' I've noticed it is hard for you when I call the register.'

- some praise: 'You tried really hard with that reading, even though it was difficult for you, well done!'
- an offer of help if the child gives up: 'Did you want to ask me for a spelling or something else?'

It is best to take the child to one side to talk to him about his problem. Opening up a relaxed dialogue about the stammer will help the child feel able to tell the teacher about his difficulties, as well as establish what the teacher can do to help. Each child who stammers will have different views on what is helpful and which situations need to be discussed.

In addition to an informal conversation about the child's difficulty, the teacher may find it useful to ask the child, if he is old enough, to write down some thoughts about his stammer perhaps on the form shown as Figure 5.4.

To my teacher _____ (teacher's name)

From _____. (name)

I want to tell you this about my problem with talking

I want to tell you this about me

When I am having trouble talking, I would like you to

When I am having trouble talking, it doesn't help when

Things I do so that people won't know about my problem

How my life would be different if I didn't have this problem

Figure 5.4 The teacher gives this sheet to the child to complete and return (see also p. 121)

Be flexible with oral tasks

Routine speaking tasks at school such as answering the register, giving his name to new adults and taking messages to other teachers can present significant difficulties for the child who stammers. In particular, registration involves a quick response in the context of the whole class listening, and this can be a source of great anxiety for a child who stammers. As his anxiety increases, so he becomes more tense and the resultant struggle to speak may appear to be highly entertaining to his classmates.

Making alternative strategies available to the whole class, such as putting up hands to answer the register, using name badges and giving written messages can save what one mother described as her child 'going through the tortures of the damned.'

STACEY
Stacey, who was seven, found it really difficult to say her name, she even asked her parents if she could change it! Her worst situation at school was when an adult (not the class teacher) asked her to say her name. Following a discussion with the class teacher it was agreed that all the children would be given a name card that they could produce when asked.

Reading aloud
If a child tends to stammer when reading aloud in a one to one setting with the teacher, it may be helpful for the teacher to read in unison with the child. This usually has the effect of making the child fluent, while still giving him the reading practice. For reading in front of the class, the teacher may try using shared reading, as defined in the Literacy Strategy, whereby the teacher reads a section to the class to demonstrate good reading technique and then reads with all the class. Furthermore, pairing the children to read in unison will help the child who stammers. Singling out the stammering child to undertake an activity differently might be rather embarrassing, so it is better to have the whole class do it differently now and again. If the child is willing to attempt a turn at reading aloud, it is helpful to ensure that the child does not have the slot to read just before break or lunchtime, when the class is anxious to finish the lesson and the child will be under pressure.

Raise awareness of all school staff

Children who stammer may experience difficulty at lunchtime or in the playground as well as in the classroom. It is therefore important that all school staff are aware that the child has this problem, and that he is not 'putting it on' or being impudent. These staff could also be informed how they can respond helpfully to the child who stammers, and strategies developed as appropriate to reduce pressures, e.g. allowing a child to point to his choice of food in the dinner queue.

TOM
Tom, aged eight, returned to the class after the lunchtime break looking very subdued. When his teacher asked him what was wrong he would say nothing, but one of the other children said that one of the lunchtime assistants had told him he did not have good manners, having failed to notice that he was blocking on 'thank you'.

Help the child to feel there is no hurry to finish speaking

It is a reality of daily life that there *is* usually a hurry to finish speaking, and the classroom is no exception to this as children clamour for one adult's attention. However, the child who stammers needs time to organise his speech and language if he is to be more fluent. This seems to be instinctively recognised, as many people instruct children who stammer to 'Slow down' or 'Take your time'.

However, slowing down the rate of talking requires self-monitoring skills that many children do not have, especially when competing with a classroom full of children. It is therefore necessary to find alternative ways to help a child to take his time to talk. The suggestions given here are similar to those in the previous chapter, with changes and additions appropriate to this age group.

Use more pauses
A useful way to create the impression that there is no hurry to speak is the use of pausing. Pausing to think before starting to talk gives the speaker time to organise his thoughts and language. The adult can model this pausing by waiting a couple of seconds before replying to a child's question, or before moving on to the next topic. The pausing can also be

accompanied by a gesture to indicate that the teacher is thinking, e.g. a finger placed on the cheek, or a verbal filler like an 'um' or 'er'

Tip: Introduce the idea of pausing to think or 'thinking time' as a topic for discussion with the whole class of children or in smaller groups.

Slow down your own speech
If somebody speaks to us in a calm and unhurried way, we are more likely to reply in similar tones. If an adult talks as slowly or even more slowly than a child who stammers, the child is more likely to be fluent.

Tip: Instead of suggesting that the child slows down when he is stammering, the adult can slow his or her own speaking rate.

Check body language
Even when an adult has slowed the pace of a conversation, it is still possible that a sense of urgency or impatience exists. It may be useful to consider if there is anything the adult is doing that could be encouraging this child to hurry up, e.g. fidgeting, doing something else at the same time, or repeatedly nodding.

Expressive language level

A child is more likely to be fluent when he is attempting a simpler, shorter sentence with familiar vocabulary. When he attempts longer, more complicated sentences with sophisticated vocabulary, his fluency skills are under greater pressure and may break down. This is even more significant for a child who has additional speech and language difficulties, e.g. delayed language development, word-finding problems and/or speech sound substitutions. It is therefore important to help the child use language that is within his capacity for fluent speech.

A teacher can influence the level of a child's linguistic responses by carefully wording questions or instructions, e.g. 'I'd like to hear something about . . .' offers a general invitation to speak, rather than 'Tell me about . . .'

This less direct approach encourages more reflection from the child and encourages engagement and interest.

Tip: The teacher's level of complexity will set the level for the children.

Encouraging turns

Most teachers implement a hand raising system in order to help children take turns to talk. This ensures that the children know that they will have a turn and that others will be quiet while they are speaking. This system is especially beneficial for the child who stammers and frequently experiences interruptions from others. However, some children also find that waiting for a turn can be anxiety provoking, so it may be helpful to give them an early turn where possible to avoid this. As before it may be simplest to ask the child what would work best.

The rules of turn taking (Appendix 5) could be discussed in the whole class and further activities to develop children's turn-taking skills are described in Chapter 7.

Build confidence

The experience of stammering can not only undermine a child's confidence as a speaker but also his self-image generally. It may therefore be important to build the child's self-esteem by focusing on his strengths so that he is able to view himself in positive terms. There are activities in Chapter 7 aimed at helping children to build a positive vocabulary that they can apply to themselves, based on specific praise, which develops their self-esteem.

In addition to the above, the child who stammers may benefit from encouragement specifically linked to speaking tasks. The class teacher or SENCO could involve the child in devising a programme of small steps to help his attempts at verbal tasks within the school setting, for example reading aloud:

1. Reading in unison
   a) with a teacher,
   b) with a friend,
   c) with a small group.
2. Reading one to one
   a) with a teacher,
   b) to a friend,
   c) with a small group.
3. Paired reading in front of the class
   a) with the teacher,
   b) with a friend.
4. Paired reading in front of school, e.g. assembly
   a) in a small group,
   b) in pairs.

The target for these activities should be to participate as best they can in a supportive environment, and success should not be dependent on fluency. As each stage is accomplished, the child could be praised in specific terms, using descriptive language such as 'brave', 'strong', and 'determined'. Thus the child will begin to view his abilities more positively and feel more confident to attempt potentially difficult speaking situations.

Children who stammer are usually fluent when singing, reading in unison, and sometimes when role playing or acting in a performance. These are good opportunities to encourage children's participation as they can enjoy the experience of being more fluent like their peers.

Disruptive behaviour and the child who stammers

Children who stammer may start to misbehave or become the class joker as it distracts attention away from their stammering problem. Some children also discover that they are more fluent when acting the clown and that they also gain in popularity as they become the focus of humour.

Collaboration between the teacher and the speech and language therapist

It is encouraging to see an increasing number of examples of successful collaboration between teachers and therapists. Where this has occurred it has been to everyone's advantage.

SLT in the community health clinic

As a result of initiatives by the British Stammering Association and SLTs, children who have fluency problems are being identified earlier and many will have been referred, assessed, and treated by an SLT before entering primary school. Some of these children will continue to need therapy while they are at school and may be seen individually or in a group (see Chapter 2 for more details). The teacher may find it helpful to use some of the checklists described in this chapter to share information with the therapist about the nature of the child's difficulties so that together they will be able to make an action plan aimed at supporting the child in school. The effect of teachers and therapists working together can be extremely powerful.

SLT working in mainstream schools

The way the services are organised will vary, but nevertheless provide the best opportunity for teachers and SLTs to work together. The consultative model and the 'pull out' system can work well for stammering children. A child may need to have individual sessions to help him understand the nature of the difficulty and methods for managing it, while planning with the teacher the ways in which the child can practise new skills in the classroom.

Children with special needs who stammer

Stammering is just as likely to affect a child with special needs, e.g. Down's Syndrome, or cerebral palsy. The same principles of management of the stammering apply if the child has special needs, and many of the recommendations will be helpful for the child's other difficulties. Sometimes, parents may focus on the stammer as one of the things that can be 'fixed'. A cautionary note, however, is that the child's level of cognitive functioning will influence his ability to monitor his own speaking skills and explore issues surrounding how his thoughts and feelings affect his stammer.

The British Stammering Association has produced a booklet entitled *Dysfluency, Stammering and Down's Syndrome* in collaboration with the Down's Syndrome Association. See the address list at the end of this book.

Teasing

Children who stammer frequently report the misery of being laughed at, mimicked, taunted and even bullied. It is an unfortunate fact that stammering is often portrayed as a joke in films and books in a way that few other problems are. Another child's instinct to giggle when he hears someone stammering may be partly a nervous response. Whatever the reason, a child who stammers will feel isolated and ridiculed and it is often in school that these situations will arise.

Many children report that their teachers are unaware of their experiences of being teased or bullied, partly because it tends to happen during breaks, or before or after school when the teachers are not present. Furthermore, teasing may be covert, in the form of sly comments which are difficult to hear, or quiet mimicking of the stammer which the busy teacher may not notice.

Schools now have Behaviour Policies for the management of bullying and the Personal, Health and Social Education

> **RYAN, ERA AND MARK**
>
> *Ryan, aged six: 'The other children keep on asking me why I talk like this, but I don't know why, so I wish they'd just leave me alone.'*
>
> *Era, aged 11: 'I'm quite clever and I usually know the answers to the teacher's questions, but when I used to put up my hand and give the answer I stammered a lot and the other children would just laugh, so now I don't put up my hand.'*
>
> *Mark, aged 33: 'My primary school days were hell: there was a group of boys in my class who used to call me M- M-Mark and take the mickey out of me constantly in the playground. I was so glad to change to secondary school, where nobody knew I stammered and from then on I learned every trick in the book to hide my problem.'*

programme provides the framework for tackling issues that surround teasing and bullying. Circle Time offers a forum for discussion and activities, as well as for dealing with specific issues that may arise within a class. The same principles apply to the subject of stammering as any other target. However, certain factors should be considered which may be specific to the problem of stammering.

'Why is he talking like that? What's wrong with him?'
Natural curiosity may prompt children to ask about stammering, and a teacher's response can establish a climate of acceptance of various differences, not only relating to speech, but also appearance, abilities etc.

Encouraging the child who stammers to tell the teacher about teasing
Talking to teachers may be especially difficult for a child who stammers; therefore it may be helpful to establish a written system of informing staff. Forms and checklists can be used with the whole class or just with certain individuals, to elicit information about teasing or bullying (Figure 5.5). An anonymous box can be set up where children can leave information about incidents that they have been involved in or witnessed (Figure 5.6).

Feedback to the child
Once a child has told the teacher about being teased, the teacher may take the appropriate action but the child may be unaware that anything has been done. This child may then be discouraged from reporting further instances as he feels nothing would change as a result. It is therefore helpful to give the child feedback about what has happened.

General checklist for whole class

Do you think that pupils are teased or bullied in this school?   Yes ☐   No ☐

If the answer is 'Yes', do you think teachers are aware of it?   Yes ☐   No ☐

Have you ever been laughed at?   Yes ☐   No ☐

      called unkind names?   Yes ☐   No ☐

      mimicked?   Yes ☐   No ☐

      threatened?   Yes ☐   No ☐

      deliberately hit/kicked/hurt?   Yes ☐   No ☐

Would you tell your teacher if someone teased/bullied you?   Yes ☐   No ☐

Would you tell your parents?   Yes ☐   No ☐

Do you have any suggestions for what the teacher could do about teasing and bullying?

Figure 5.5   A form which can be given to all the children (see also p. 122)

There are many useful publications on the management of bullying in schools. The British Stammering Association publishes a programme for the management of bullying in primary schools.

I want to tell you what happened to me

This is how I have been teased or bullied (It's OK to use the exact words that were said)

This is how I reacted

This is what happened next

This is how the teasing/bullying made me feel

This is what I would like to be done about it

Any other comments

Figure 5.6   A form for individual children (see also p. 123)

What will happen to the child's stammer in future?

While some primary school children do overcome the stammer, for others a more realistic aim will be for them to learn to live with the problem, and find ways to manage themselves with confidence in spite of the stammer. Without help the stammer may dominate the child's life, emotionally, socially and educationally. The child's thinking may become ruled by the fear of stammering and how people might react to it.

Help for the young child who stammers is generally aimed at the parents as well as the child. However, as the child gets older, the focus is more upon the child learning to manage his problem. Clinical experience suggests that at this age the parents are often more concerned about the stammering than the children. This can be extremely frustrating for the parents because if the child does not wish to tackle the problem, there is unlikely to be much progress. It is usually more appropriate to wait until the child is motivated to do something about his speech.

It is helpful if parents or teachers indicate on the application form that a child has a stammer and whether or not he is receiving speech and language therapy. This ensures that secondary school staff, especially the child's form tutor, will be prepared for the child. It may also be useful to include information about strategies the child and teachers have devised which have helped the child manage in a variety of situations, e.g. registration, oral tasks, teasing etc.

If the child is required to attend for an interview, he may benefit from some preparation and possibly practice, either at home or in school. Again, it would be beneficial if those interviewing the child were informed in advance that he has a stammering problem.

Transfer to secondary school

Summary

Each child who stammers does so in his own unique style and will have different needs in terms of how he is supported at school. However, the demands of a busy classroom are such that individual management plans, especially those requiring extra time for an individual, can be impractical. If the child does not have an Individual Education Plan (IEP), the teacher should ask advice of the SENCO. Teachers are not speech and language therapists (nor vice versa), they have different roles. But with a collaborative approach between the teacher, the child, his parents, and the speech and language therapist, the child who stammers can be helped within the classroom using some of the suggestions outlined above.

Chapter 6

The secondary school student

It is well recognised that a student's secondary school years mark a period of great change. The pressures of rapid physiological and psychological growth make this a difficult and often turbulent time. Furthermore the influential role of the family lessens as the student moves through adolescence and towards increasing independence. For the student who stammers, transferring to secondary school presents the challenges of a new environment, the pressures of adolescence and the complex difficulties associated with persistent stammering. Furthermore, it is at a time when the curricular demands on communication skills are formalising and will be eventually assessed at sophisticated levels for the GCSEs and 'A' Levels or equivalent examinations across the United Kingdom.

This chapter will describe the changes that can occur in stammering behaviour during secondary school years and the impact this may have on other aspects of students' lives. It will help teachers recognise the additional problems that may arise for students who stammer, particularly in relation to their academic performance and social inclusion. Practical suggestions are made for the management of stammering in the classroom, dealing with the demands of the curriculum and preparation for leaving school.

Introduction

How is the problem highlighted for staff?

On transfer to secondary school, the records from previous schools are passed on and it is usually the role of the Special Educational Needs Coordinator (SENCO) to disseminate information throughout the school about a pupil who

Identifying a stammering problem

stammers. This role is particularly complex in a secondary school where the number of subject, support and ancillary staff will be very large, and will also include supply staff who may only be in school on a short-term basis. The SENCO may find it helpful to provide some information about the nature of stammering, such as the British Stammering Association's (BSA) leaflets for schools (see Useful Addresses at the end of this book).

There are, however, many students who stammer who are not on the special needs register and will not be known to the SENCO. In this case, parents may alert staff to a problem by talking to the head of year and the form tutor at a 'new parents' evening and request that any relevant information will be distributed throughout the school. However, in some cases students who stammer may remain undetected for some time.

What are the signs and symptoms of stammering in older pupils?

Most of these students will have been stammering for some time so the difficulties they are experiencing are often wider ranging, more firmly entrenched and increasingly resistant to change. Their heightened self-consciousness and awareness of others may also result in increasing frustration, embarrassment, and lack of confidence.

The stammer may involve overt behaviours such as repetitions, prolongations and blocks and also covert behaviours such as avoidance strategies. Teachers may find it useful to refer to the detailed descriptions of the types of stammering behaviour in Chapter 5, together with the 'Describing the stammer' checklist in Appendix 6.

Coping and avoidance strategies
The feelings of embarrassment and the fear of stammering are likely to intensify with the severity of the symptoms and this often leads to students using avoidance strategies to disguise the stammer. They may also use a variety of 'tactics ' that help them get through difficult moments. For example, they may use extra words as 'starters and fillers' such as 'y' know', 'right', 'kind of' etc., they may change words around or substitute a difficult word with one they find easier to say, even if the meaning is compromised. Sometimes they will even give an incorrect answer rather than risk stammering on the correct one, they may pretend not to have heard the question, or distract people's attention away from their speech. Some pupils become so anxious that they will avoid speaking at all

whenever they can, and others may go to extreme lengths to avoid situations altogether.

> **PETER**
> *Peter was fifteen and had a marked stammer. When he was faced with a situation such as speaking in front of the class, his fear of 'getting completely stuck' would cause him to become so disruptive in the class that the teacher would send him out and, much to his relief, he would miss his turn.*

The avoidance of words and situations may become a well-rehearsed and highly complex strategy, so that the student may be able to disguise the extent of the problem, both at home and in school.

> **GARY**
> *Gary was fourteen and had stammered for many years. However, he had a good vocabulary and was so skilled at changing 'difficult' words that nobody at school had any idea there was a problem with his speech.*

Some pupils find that they can be fluent with quick asides, wisecracks and swearing, and may take on a role as the 'class joker', which not only distracts attention away from the stammer but can also make them popular with their peers.

These strategies may seem helpful to the student in the short term but can take a great deal of mental energy, become emotionally and physically exhausting, and create as many difficulties as they resolve.

The social and emotional effects of stammering

The constant fear of being identified as having a stammer may begin to have an effect on a student's developing relationships with his peers. These students may be reluctant to talk for fear of stammering and so appear shy and difficult to get to know. If they communicate despite the stammer they risk being stereotyped, ridiculed or teased. The reactions of peers and teachers can make the difference between a student who gradually feels confident enough to participate in the life of the school, or one who feels increasingly anxious about speaking and becomes withdrawn and isolated.

The previous chapter referred to the positive and negative cycles which illustrate how a person's thinking affects their feelings, which then changes their physical state and finally the stammering itself (see Appendix 8).

> **CLAIRE**
>
> *Twelve-year-old Claire explained, 'Once I realised that people at school knew I stammered and they didn't seem to take much notice of it, I stopped worrying about my speech so much, and from that moment on it started to get better.'*
>
> *Therapy helped Claire to understand how her thoughts affected her stammering and she was then able to become more realistic in the way she thought and felt about herself and the stammer.*

> **CRAIG**
>
> *Craig at fifteen described his inability to talk to girls because he knew he would stammer, which would make them laugh at him and think he was stupid. He described getting so tense that his stomach would knot thinking about it. If he did pluck up the courage, he stammered so badly that he wished he hadn't, so he usually 'bottled out', and then felt enormous frustration and loss of confidence. Craig was locked into a negative cycle that resulted in him stammering or avoiding the situation altogether.*

In some extreme cases, the feelings of shame and consequent loss of confidence have resulted in young people becoming so isolated that they become depressed and occasionally have suicidal thoughts.

Which situations are difficult?

There is considerable variation in the situations that present difficulty to pupils who stammer. Teachers therefore may find it helpful to use the checklist 'When is he stammering?' in Appendix 7 to guide their observations.

> **JOHN**
>
> *John had disguised his stammer at school by not saying very much and avoiding words he found difficult. Sometimes he felt able to answer questions and he would put his hand up in class, which made him feel good. However, on a 'bad' day, when his speech was much more difficult, he would keep very quiet but dread classes where the teacher might ask questions at random. He said he was constantly terrified that he would make a fool of himself.*

There are certain classroom situations that these students find especially difficult to handle; registration; speaking in front of a group; reading aloud; explaining complex ideas; oral class work; speaking under time pressure; waiting for their turn; being laughed at or teased; or talking to teachers or other authority figures.

> **MELISSA**
> *Melissa was approaching her oral examination in French and was convinced that she would get completely stuck and be unable to continue. She was terrified of making an idiot of herself, and that the teacher would think she was stupid. She thought she would fail, and knew she ought to talk to the teacher. Melissa had never mentioned her stammer to anyone, not even her parents who thought she had grown out of it, so the thought of having to tell the teacher made her feel extremely anxious. She finally plucked up courage, and told her teacher about her difficulty. The teacher was very helpful, encouraging and supportive and together they worked out how to get the extra practice she needed to cope with the examination.*

What teachers can do to help

As secondary school pupils become increasingly independent, they can be encouraged to work out for themselves how they would like teachers to support them with their difficulties.

The previous chapter will answer many of the questions teachers may have about what they should do when talking to a student who stammers.

In brief the general advice is to:

- Wait and give him time to speak.
- Give the same eye contact as you would a fluent student.
- Try not to hurry him.
- Speak in a calm, unhurried manner.
- Resist the temptation to guess the word for him.

It can be helpful to see the student on his own to acknowledge the problem and discuss what would be helpful. Occasionally there are students who find it easier to communicate in writing. Teachers could consider using the form 'To my teacher' in Appendix 9 for younger students whereas older students may prefer to write down the situations that they find difficult and suggest ways the teachers could help. This can open the lines of communication and make it possible for an ongoing discussion between the student and the teacher.

Communicate information with all members of staff

Many of the problems that arise for students in school can be attributed simply to lack of awareness. In many cases the teachers simply did not know the student had a stammer. Although it is difficult to ensure that all members of staff (including ancillary staff) receive information, it could make a significant difference to the student who stammers. A meeting could also be arranged involving the student who stammers, his parents, the SENCO or form tutor and the speech and language therapist where it is appropriate. The difficulties the student is experiencing can then be discussed and strategies for managing these put forward, with the student being encouraged and supported in choosing options that could be tried out.

Build flexibility into class procedures

As previously discussed, class procedures such as registration, supplying names and information, reading aloud and answering questions can present particular difficulties for the pupil who stammers.

- *Registration*: Most students want to be treated like all the other pupils especially if they feel confident that they will be given time to respond. Others may find that giving their name or address is particularly difficult and may benefit from having an alternative strategy such as raising a hand, writing down details of name and address etc. for lists. If a substitute teacher is in charge of the class, a seating plan may help so that pupils do not have to give their name although seating arrangements are not always fixed in secondary school classrooms.
- *Reading aloud*: Asking for volunteers can make this situation much easier for the student who stammers, as he will be able to participate on days when his speech is easier to manage and not on other days.

  When the exercise is part of the curriculum experience, as in English lessons, pupils could be given prior notice so that they can practise reading the text in advance. It may also be helpful to give the student the opportunity to discuss when he would prefer to be called upon to read. Some find that going first enables them to be more fluent than waiting for their turn. Paired or small group reading could be encouraged in the class, as pupils who stammer will usually be able to be quite fluent when reading in unison with others. As discussed earlier it is most helpful for pupils who stammer to be involved with the teacher in resolving the difficulties presented by these situations.

- *Question and answer sessions*: While many pupils who stammer find it harder to answer questions that come without warning, there are some who find it easier because they have no time to become anxious. In general therefore, operating a system where pupils volunteer to answer questions will allow them the best opportunity to respond when they feel able to. When a pupil has had difficulty answering a question but managed to get through it, the teacher could help by drawing attention to the value of its contents.

Increase confidence and self-esteem

Developing confidence is important for many young people but often it seems to be particularly difficult to achieve during adolescence. Appropriate praise and reinforcement is the most productive way of increasing self-esteem, and parents and teachers have a clear role here. However, as they get older the students also need to learn to reinforce *themselves*: discovering ways of 'patting themselves on the back' for achievements, rather than putting themselves down and undermining their own attempts to progress. This could be tackled in the Personal, Health, and Social Education programme (PHSE). There is no doubt that the more confident a pupil is the more likely they are to be able to manage their speech difficulty successfully.

See Chapter 7 for practical exercises.

Managing teasing and bullying

Children who stammer may be particularly vulnerable to teasing and bullying. This was demonstrated by a survey of adult members of the British Stammering Association, in which 82 per cent reported they were bullied in school and 14.93 per cent of those reported that the bullying was related to their stammer (Mooney and Smith 1995). All state schools now have a Behaviour Policy, and that may include an anti-bullying policy which is disseminated to parents, so that everyone is clear about the procedures that are in place.

Most strategies rely on the child telling an adult about the bullying. As some pupils who stammer have difficulties with this, systems that allow written reports of bullying can be helpful. The forms in Appendix 10 and Appendix 11 may be useful for some students.

The school's PHSE programme has an important role to play in creating a school climate where diversity is accepted. Some students may feel able to talk to their class about their stammer in the context of such a programme, others may find this too difficult.

Appointing a mentor

Some schools adopt a system in which students are assigned to a named teacher or other adult who offers support. The student may have regular appointments when he meets up with the mentor to discuss how he is getting on and any problems which may have arisen. This role of mentor may provide continuity of support as the pupil progresses through the school.

Strategies for English oral examinations

Oral examination tasks will vary with the individual practices of the school and the selected board, but in general they are likely to include a discussion with another pupil, a group discussion, and a presentation to an audience. Pupils are required to communicate ideas to the audience, using appropriate language, register, tone, vocabulary and pace. Early planning and practice for these tasks will be especially helpful to students who stammer.

As schools undertake the oral assessments, there is the opportunity for flexibility in order to provide support for a pupil who stammers:

- Students may be encouraged to present a talk measured in number of words rather than length of time. Pupils who stammer become much more anxious when constrained by time limits, whereas a word limit allows them to take their time for the delivery, whereby they are more likely to be fluent.
- Oral assessments may be based upon situations outside the English classroom.

STEVEN
Steven, who stammered severely in the English classroom when giving a talk, was able to present a talk about his football team's performance to the Year Seven team which he was helping to coach. He became so engaged in the content that he hardly stammered at all.

Strategies for modern language oral examinations

It may be helpful to encourage students to:

- Plan and prepare ahead, as this helps some students perform more fluently.
- Use a tape recorder to practise using the language, and to monitor their rate of speech and other communication skills.
- Work with a conversation 'buddy' to practise their skills.
- Plan vocabulary and content for the oral.
- Memorise material or use prompt cards if the student finds that helpful.
- Use audio-visual aids and/handouts.
- Apply for special consideration where appropriate.

If the student attends speech and language therapy, the therapist may help in the planning and practice of oral examinations.

Special consideration
The examination boards may grant this if there is sufficient evidence to show that the pupil needs support to access the modern language curriculum. In the case of a young person who stammers, completing an oral piece in a set time may cause considerable anxiety and stress, thereby undermining his performance. The school can apply for special consideration for a pupil who stammers if these criteria can be met. Usually the Board will require supporting evidence from a professional before considering the application, in this case the speech and language therapist. Applications for special consideration are made simpler if the pupil has been placed on the special needs register for two years before the application. However, practice over these issues does vary with exam boards and individual schools. If appropriate, the school could discuss the matter with the pupil and parents at the beginning of the examination curriculum, and make a preliminary enquiry to the examining board for advice.

Should the board grant special consideration, then the usual practice for modern languages is to allow extra time, on average twenty-five minutes. The certificate will indicate with a symbol that special consideration has been awarded.

Occasionally the British Stammering Association has been approached by schools, therapists or parents asking for advice on how the oral component may be avoided altogether as a student has become so distressed. The procedures are similar to those requesting special consideration. In these cases the student would only be assessed on the components presented for examination and the certificate would indicate that there was no oral component presented for assessment.

Work experience

A carefully chosen placement can have a significant and positive effect on a student's confidence. The teacher and student should consider a wide a range of options based on the student's skills and interests rather than on his speech. It is important however to encourage the student to inform the employer about his stammer so that both parties feel comfortable discussing any difficulties if they should arise. Furthermore it has been noted by students that once they have disclosed the stammer they become more relaxed and often stammer less.

Further education and careers

Careers teachers, careers guidance officers and parents should encourage students who stammer to consider as many opportunities as if the student were fluent. It may be tempting to assume there are professions that are closed to people who stammer.

> **BARRY**
> *Barry, aged 27, was going to be best man at a wedding and had to make a speech. He was very nervous about it and frightened he might stammer. When asked about his job, he revealed he was an air traffic controller! He went on to say that when he was at work ' I never stammer then, there's far too much to think about!'*

Furthermore the Disability and Discrimination Act (1995) is impacting upon the provision made by employers for people with a disability, and they are obliged to find strategies to support them. This should allow the student to consider as many options as any other pupil.

Completing application forms
It is helpful to discuss with the student what information to give the college or employer about the stammer. Students are sometimes reluctant to do this and may need help to present it in a positive light, e.g. 'I have a stammer, but I don't let it interfere with what I want to say.' Once the student has

acknowledged the stammer, it often has a positive effect on the speech at any subsequent interview.

References
Teachers writing a reference should be encouraged to discuss the positive aspects of the student's communication skills, and refer to the stammer in this context.

Interviews
As stated above, if the student is aware that the interviewer knows about his stammer, it may take some of the anxiety out of the situation and help him to be more fluent. In addition, interviewers may be more lenient with time and may put the student more at ease if they are prepared in advance.

Some guidelines:

- Students can be encouraged to talk about their stammer at the interview if they feel able to, as this demonstrates a mature and thoughtful approach to the problem. It also often has the effect of reducing anxiety and improving their performance.

> **MIKE**
> *Mike was applying to medical school. He had a stammer that could be severe when he was anxious. He discussed his application with the careers officer and decided it was important to talk about his speech. When he subsequently went to interview he was astonished to find that one of the interviewers, a doctor, had a stammer. Mike is now studying medicine.*

- Students should be encouraged to prepare thoroughly for interviews anticipating questions and planning replies.
- Mock interviews can be very helpful. The student should be encouraged to identify all the positive aspects of their performance and build on these.

Collaboration between teachers and speech and language therapists

In these circumstances communication between professionals is the key to success.

SLT in the community health centre
Some pupils will be attending therapy locally, either in a small group or perhaps in individual sessions (see Chapter 2 for

further details). Setting up a meeting in school or over the phone will provide an opportunity for the therapist to share information from the assessments that will provide insight into the difficulties the student may be experiencing in school. The SENCO or form tutor (as it would usually be one of these figures in a secondary school setting) may also be able to seek advice about specific curriculum-based problems for a student. There may also be a number of ways in which they can support therapy within the school environment. In secondary schools, SENCOs do most liaison and dissemination of SEN information.

SLT working in mainstream schools
The service provided will vary considerably across the United Kingdom. However, where possible the teacher and the SLT could collaborate in the assessment of a pupil's communication using some of the tools described in this chapter. Further joint planning of targets and strategies with the student will provide a solid basis for collaboration. Some services may also be able to offer the student some individual sessions for specific targets.

CLAIRE
Claire was very worried about an interview for a place at university. The therapist organised some individual sessions which culminated in a videotaped mock interview. When it was over Claire left the room in tears, so disappointed was she about her speech performance. However, when she saw the video she realised she had hardly stammered at all and in all other respects she had presented herself extremely well.

Summary The principle difference in the management of this age group is that it becomes increasingly important *not* to tell the students what to do but to help them work it out for themselves. Furthermore, both the students and the teachers need to understand that the fear of stammering is as big a problem as the stammer itself, and that the negative feelings and attitudes that are a part of the fear are very damaging to the individual. Where possible the teacher and the pupil need to work together to understand the particular difficulties he faces and then to negotiate an action plan for all concerned.

There is no doubt that a teacher who understands the difficulties faced by students who stammer will be able to play a vital role in helping such students to participate in all aspects of their education.

Chapter 7

Social communication skills and stammering

Introduction

Stammering and the social context are mutually dependent. The responses of others are as important as the problem itself. Throughout childhood and adolescence the person who stammers may have developed strategies and techniques to minimise, disguise or hide the problem. These can adversely affect the development of social interaction skills and add to the difficulty in communicating effectively.

Therefore therapy will often focus on helping young people who stammer to be more socially skilled and confident across a range of situations.

Social communication skills in school

The publication of new guidelines for education, which identify speaking and listening as key skills, emphasises the importance of helping students to develop their overall communication skills within the school environment. Given the wealth of available social skills resources tailored specifically to the classroom, this chapter has three aims. Firstly, it will hope to emphasise the similarity of targets between the classroom and speech and language therapy and therefore the possibilities for professional collaboration and partnership. Secondly, it offers a hierarchy of communication skills and a process for developing them which may be useful. Some exercises and activities are described to illustrate how the framework may be used with different age groups. Finally, it will clarify the particular relevance of social skills work to stammering.

A communication skills hierarchy

The following activities help pupils to observe, listen, take turns, give and receive positive reinforcement or praise, problem solve and negotiate, while also encouraging them to discuss their ideas and feelings more effectively. The activities progress from simple to more complex communication skills following the hierarchy developed by Rustin (1987), and it is recommended that they are presented in the following order:

1. Observation and eye contact
2. Listening
3. Turn taking
4. Praise and reinforcement
5. Problem solving
6. Negotiation

Activities for each skill are presented in an order suitable for younger to older pupils. A useful sequence for each successive skill can be as follows:

1. Introduce the topic with an activity for raising awareness.
2. Brainstorm the topic in order to elaborate and develop understanding of the concept.
3. Encourage discussion in order to expand and share ideas.
4. Practise and consolidate through further activities.

Brainstorming

Brainstorming engages pupils' interest, encourages their active involvement, demonstrates the value of their own ideas and reinforces the personal relevance of a topic. The brainstorm topics help children to identify why each skill is important both to themselves and to others, to consider the implications when the skill is not used, and the benefits that may come from practising it more often. Importantly, brainstorming helps children to develop their empathy with others, an important aspect of social competence.

Reminders for running brainstorming sessions

1. Explain that the aim of brainstorming is to generate as many ideas as possible on a given topic.
2. Outline the following rules:
   - Aim for as many ideas as possible.

- Do not judge the ideas as they are offered. All ideas are accepted and included.
- Build on and expand others' ideas.

3. Write the topic at the top of the board and write all ideas underneath.

4. Use the pupil's own words

5. Have key ideas in mind along with prompt questions which can help less confident students to contribute.

Introducing communication skills

Brainstorm topics: 'What is good communication?'
'What skills do we need to be good communicators?'

The main aim is to orientate the students to the general topic and to encourage them to consider what good communication means and what it involves. Key areas that will be introduced later may be elicited if necessary through further prompts. The complexity of communication becomes evident through this brainstorming, and the importance of non-verbal as well as verbal aspects made clear.

Observation and eye contact

Learning to use appropriate eye contact and being generally observant about others is an integral part of effective communication. Observation helps individuals to be more aware of how others are feeling; it develops their sense of empathy and helps them to contribute appropriately to conversations. Similarly, using appropriate eye contact helps individuals to show their interest in the other person, which reinforces conversations and therefore relationships. People who stammer frequently look away during moments of dysfluency because of self-consciousness, embarrassment, or concern about how others will react to the stammer. In turn, this can be misinterpreted as lack of interest by others and, importantly, prevents the person who stammers from observing how people are in fact responding. While people who stammer may encounter negative and inappropriate responses from others, by not looking they also miss positive responses as well. Students who stammer may be encouraged to give appropriate eye contact by being in an environment where the class as a whole is aware of this skill and is encouraged. It should be noted that there are cultural differences in the use of eye contact and that appropriate eye contact never means an unremitting gaze.

Activities to raise awareness

All activities are coded as suitable for: E = Early years; P = Primary school; S = Secondary school.

Gestures (E, P)
The teacher tells the children to copy his or her actions, then puts hands on head, crosses legs, folds arms, etc. and the children copy. The teacher then tells the children to close their eyes and still copy the actions. The children realise they cannot copy actions without looking. The teacher explains how we often find out what people want us to do by watching their actions, as well as by listening to them.

Emotions (E, P)
The teacher makes a statement and the children have to guess how the teacher is feeling by the expression on his or her face. For example, the teacher says 'I am going to have lunch'; keeping the intonation pattern the same she changes her facial expression, smiling and looking happy, and then repeats the phrase looking sad, then scared. The children identify each feeling that the teacher is expressing. The teacher then asks the children to cover their eyes and repeats the exercise, but the children discover they cannot tell how the teacher is feeling if they are not looking at her face.

Brainstorming

'Why is looking/observation important in good communication?'

Example (with a class of seven year olds)
'So you know it is your turn to talk.'
'People will think you are rude if you don't look.'
'You can tell what people are like.'
'You can tell how someone is feeling.'
'They might not hear you if they are not looking.'

Discussion points/prompts

'How do you feel when you're talking to someone and they don't look at you?'
'What can you learn about other people by looking at them?'

Activities for further practice

Follow me (E, P)
The teacher performs an action, e.g. hands on head, and the children are to copy that action. The teacher changes the action and the children follow suit. Children who are not watching and keeping up with changes are encouraged to look more closely.

What has gone? (E, P)
Several objects are placed on a tray and named. The children then close their eyes and the teacher removes one of the objects. The children open their eyes and they are asked what has been taken.

What is different? (E, P)
The children are told to look carefully at the teacher and notice everything about what he or she looks like. They are then told to close their eyes and the teacher changes one aspect of their appearance, e.g. removes a shoe. The children then open their eyes and identify what has changed. This can be made more difficult by changing two things.

'Noticing' (E, P, S)
In pairs the children are asked to go out at playtime and notice something the other children are doing that is unusual or interesting. Older students could report back to the class an example of someone using a communication skill to good effect and an example of one that did not work so well.

Looking stars (E, P)
Stars are awarded during each day, or during a particular time during the day, for looking and eye contact.

'Who am I talking to?' (E, P)
The teacher tells the children that she is going to ask each of them to do something, e.g. put their hands on their head. The first time she will call a child by name, the rest of the time she will indicate just by looking them in the eye who the instruction is for. The teacher then looks at another child and, without using their name, asks them to perform an action.

Eye contact to indicate turns (E, P)
The teacher explains that he or she will indicate whose turn it is to do something by looking at them, e.g. when it is time to find their coat, the teacher looks at a child and that child knows it is their turn to get their coat.

Swapping chairs (E, P)
With the class seated in a circle, the teacher explains that she will swap places with the child that she looks at next. The teacher then looks at one of the children and swaps places with them. The teacher can instruct other children to be the 'lookers' who will also look at another child and then swap places with them.

Change three things (P, S)
The students stand in pairs facing each other. They take it in turns to first observe their partner for a few moments then they turn away while their partner changes three things about themselves, and then turn back to identify the changes that have been made. Changes can be made to facial expression, stance, and something more general such as altering jewellery or clothing.

Listening

As children become more aware of stammering, they can develop a range of strategies in an attempt to manage the problem more effectively. Some of these can be unhelpful as they disrupt other communication skills and may actually contribute to self-consciousness. Frequently older students will explain that they rehearse what they are going to say, or scan ahead and change those words which they think will be difficult. Strategies such as these lessen the degree to which the student is able to listen to the other(s) in the conversation, and as a result they then may feel even less able to contribute as they lose the thread of the conversation. The following activities cover related aspects of listening, including ignoring background noise, sequencing skills and memory.

Activities for raising awareness

Spot the mistake (E, P)
This activity raises awareness by focusing on the implications of not listening. The teacher asks a question and then responds inappropriately to the reply given.

Example: *Teacher:* 'What did you have for breakfast today?'
          Child: 'I had toast'.
          Teacher: ' Oh you had *cereal?* . . . Did you have Frosties?'

By 'playing dumb' the teacher can get the class to tell her what to do differently.

Role play good and bad listening (E, P, S)
The teacher and a helper role play good listening and bad listening in a variety of ways, e.g. talking at the same time as each other, looking out of the window, fidgeting.

'Can you hear me?' (E, P)
The teacher tells all the children to recite a nursery rhyme and while they are doing so the teacher, using a quiet voice, asks them to stand up. Most of the children will not have listened to the instruction, so the teacher repeats it more and more loudly until all the children are standing. The group then discusses the need to listen carefully when there is other noise in the room.

'How many can you do?' (E, P)
The teacher invites a child to perform an action, e.g. clap your hands. The teacher then asks another child to perform two actions, e.g. stand up and put your hands on your head. The teacher continues to ask children to do things, increasing the number of actions until it becomes too difficult for the children to remember the whole instruction. The group then discusses the importance of listening *and* remembering what they have heard.

Brainstorming

'Why is listening important?'
'What's involved in good listening?'

Example (with a class of 15 year olds)
'It reinforces the speaker.'
'You know what the conversation is about.'
'You know what to say next.'
'It shows you are interested.'
'It shows respect.'
'If people don't listen, you have to repeat things, that's boring.'
'The conversation breaks down if you don't listen.'
'If someone doesn't listen, you lose respect for them and get angry.'
'It makes you feel bad when people don't listen.'

Discussion points/prompts

'How do you feel when people don't listen to you?'
'How do you feel when someone listens to you carefully?'
'What can make it difficult to listen?'

Activities for further practice

Musical actions (E, P)
Match each of a range of musical instruments to an action. For example when the maraca is shaken everyone is to stand up, when the bell is rung they are to put their hands on their knees, when the whistle is blown they are to stand on one leg etc. Start with one instrument only, with the children listening and performing the correct action. Increase to two or more instruments in sequence in order to build up the children's listening, memory and sequencing skills.

Animal story (E, P)
Explain that during the following story about animals their task is to make the right sound for each animal when it is mentioned. The sound effects may need to be established first. The children are then told to listen carefully as the teacher tells the story so that they make the right animal sounds at the right time. The same activity can be carried out using a transport story, e.g. trains, cars, planes, or a story involving musical instruments.

Chinese whispers (E, P)
The teacher gives a message to one child in a group, either seated around a table or standing in a line. The child whispers the message to the person next to them and so on down the line until the last person delivers the message back to the teacher. The class can then discuss what happened to the message for the listener and the speaker and its implications.

Listening pictures (E, P)
Photographs taken in the classroom, assembly or playground which show children both listening and not listening, or pictures collected from other sources are used to make a collage, poster or scrap book illustrating the nonverbal aspects of listening.

'How well did we listen?' (P, S)
This could also be used as a way of reinforcing the information a teacher has given in a lesson. Small groups get together afterwards and piece together all the things they can remember to tell back to the whole group to see which group remembers the most.

'I went to market' (P, S)
An alternative version of this well known listening and memory game is 'I went on holiday and I took a . . .' These

activities can be helped by each student miming an action to go with their chosen item.

Tell a story (P, S)
In small groups, one person recounts an incident that has happened to them in real life. A second person listens and then retells the story as closely as they can to the original. The rest of the group listens to both and makes a judgement about how well the listener retold the story, and fills in the bits that were left out. Following this, a discussion should be encouraged in order to elaborate the role and value of this skill and also to identify the things that interfere with good listening. Pictures or storyboards help younger pupils with this activity.

Turn taking

As described earlier, children who stammer, as well as those with a range of other communication difficulties, sometimes find it difficult to participate and take turns in a conversation. Where turn taking is compromised, for example by pupils interrupting each other, there is increased pressure to formulate ideas quickly and to respond rapidly. This implicit time pressure is unhelpful for individuals who stammer, particularly when they are attempting to use strategies to give them more control of their fluency, or when they need more time to formulate what they wish to say. Alternatively, when the environment is one in which people listen to one another and wait for others to finish, there is less time pressure, which helps the stammering child to maximise his or her fluency. It is therefore helpful when the class as a whole establishes, and keeps to, rules about taking turns and not interrupting each other. The convention of students raising their hands to indicate that they have something to say while someone else is talking is a helpful, concrete way to practise turn taking.

Activities to raise awareness

'What just happened?' (E, P, S)
This involves making the most of examples of poor turn taking as they arise in order to increase pupils' awareness and self-monitoring and to help them elaborate their understanding of what can go wrong with turn taking and what effect this has. The following questions can be useful:

'What happened when I asked the question?'
'How many children tried to answer at the same time?'

'What happens to your voice when you are trying to say something at the same time as somebody else?'
'What happens when everybody starts to speak louder?'
'How many children can I listen to at one time?'

Use of video (P, S)
There are many instances of poor turn taking on television and watching recorded dialogues can help pupils identify problems and consequences in the same way as above.

Role play (E, P, S)
The teacher and another helper role-play poor turn taking skills. During a few minutes of conversation they constantly overlap and interrupt one another so that neither of them is able to finish what they are trying to say. The pupils are then asked to comment on what is going wrong and how turn taking could be improved.

Breaking into the conversation (P, S)
The class is divided into groups of threes. Two students in each group are instructed to have a conversation for three minutes with each other and deliberately exclude the third person. The third person is instructed to try and break into the conversation in some way, and the other two try not to let him/her.

Brainstorming

'Why is turn taking important in the classroom?'
'What do we need to do to be good at turn taking?'

Discussion points/prompts

'How do you feel when you don't get your turn to speak?'
'How do you feel when someone interrupts you?'
'How might other people feel when they're interrupted?'

Activities for further practice

Pass the hat (E, P)
The teacher explains that a hat will be placed on someone's head to indicate that it is their turn to speak. A verbal game is played, e.g. 'My favourite food is . . .'. The child wearing the hat has his or her turn and then places the hat on another child's head. That child has his or her turn and puts the hat on another child's head, until everyone has had a turn.

Build a story (E, P)

This exercise may be carried out in a large group or in several smaller groups.

Each group is instructed that they are to make up a story in their group. One pupil will start the story with an opening sentence, e.g. 'A boy called Tim was about to go on holiday...' Each pupil in turn adds a sentence, following the theme of the story, until everybody has contributed.

Group rules (E, P, S)

The class is encouraged to develop rules that everyone feels would be helpful within the classroom, drawing on ideas from turn taking in games if necessary. The following ideas are likely to be included:

Listen so we know what others are saying and when they have finished.

Look at the other speaker so we know when they are expecting us to say something (explain to the children that when we have finished what we want to say, we usually look at the other person to indicate that it is their turn).

Wait until the other person has completely finished even if we think we know what they are going to say.

Turn taking should be fair. Everyone should have an opportunity to speak which may include encouraging more reluctant members of the group.

Don't carry on too long. The speaker must be aware that they should stop to let another person have their turn to talk.

The microphone game (E, P, S).

A group of children is instructed that they will take part in an activity in which they will all take turns to speak. A microphone (which may be real or represented by a pencil or ruler etc.) will be held by the child whose turn it is to speak and this will show the others that they should not interrupt. When each child has finished his or her turn they put the microphone down so that the next person can speak. Everybody should have a turn with the microphone and none of the turns should be too long. It is also the responsibility of the group to ensure that everyone does indeed have a turn. The verbal activity can be fairly simple for very young children to start with, e.g. each person in the group says, ' My favourite food is . . .' or ' I am wearing a . . .'. Once they have the idea the same principle can be applied to telling or re-telling stories. It may be helpful to appoint a new turn taking monitor each time who will make sure that the rules they established are being kept. This activity gives the children a concrete reminder of the process of turn taking. The concept of the microphone can then be used to remind children to take turns at other times when the actual microphone is not being used, e.g. 'Sam, who has the microphone?'

Turn taking in the class room (P, S)
The children are asked to notice over the day how much of the following they do during a day:

Talking?
Listening?
Interrupting?

This task can be discussed within the class at the end of the day. The students then brainstorm ideas about how they might encourage better turn taking in the class and produce an action plan for the next day.

Praise and reinforcement

As has been identified throughout this book, students who stammer are often described by their parents as lacking in confidence and self-esteem, and this becomes more evident as they become increasingly aware of the difference between their abilities and those of their more fluent peers. Furthermore, they tend to stammer more when they feel less confident, and less when they feel more confident. The main source of a child's confidence is the verbal and nonverbal encouragement received from significant adults. Faber and Mazlish (1987), in their book for parents, advocate a focused and structured approach to reinforcing children's behaviour, which we have adapted, and which involves the following steps:

1. Describe what you have noticed, e.g. 'Well done, Moshe, you put all your things away in the cupboard.'

2. Add a word which describes a relevant attribute that the child can begin to apply to him/herself, e.g. 'That was very helpful (responsible, thoughtful, organised etc.) of you.'

This detailed and specific form of praise gives children more information about what they have done that was appreciated instead of the more general 'Well done' or 'Good boy/girl.' Another example might be, 'Thank you, Karl, for taking care of Julie when she fell in the playground. That was very thoughtful of you.' Praise that is specific and descriptive helps children to develop a positive vocabulary which builds confidence and self-esteem. Appropriate reinforcement received from peers and the ability to self-reinforce are particularly helpful for students.

Brainstorming

'Why is praise important in good communication?'

Example (from a class of nine year olds)
'People treat each other better.'
'It makes people happy.'
'It stops bullying.'
'It helps friendships.'
'It shows that people like you.'
'You can learn something from being praised.'
'It makes you feel warm inside.'
'Your heart would break without praise.'
'It doesn't matter what is on the outside, it is on the inside that is important.'
'People will praise you back.'
'You feel more confident.'
'Without it you feel lonely.'

Discussion points/prompts

'What skills do we need to be able to praise people?'
> (Observation, eye contact.)

'How should praise be given?'
> (Say it genuinely, honestly, look at the person, don't laugh, can be about small things as well as big things.)

'When someone praises us what should we do?'
> (Say 'thank you', smile, look at the person.)
> Note: it may be a useful discussion point to consider the more 'usual' reactions of – ignoring it, laughing, minimising it and why these can be unhelpful, e.g. 'How might the other person feel if you laugh when they have praised you?'

Activities for further practice

Praise presents (P)
Children are familiar with presents and understand how to give and receive them. It may be helpful for children to think of praise in the same way they do a present.

Teachers and helpers think of something they wish to praise each child for and using the model described earlier write it down on a piece of paper, e.g. 'You helped Kate when she had lost her book – that was very helpful of you'. Make each one into a parcel by folding over several times, and hand it to the child, who should read it and say thank you.

Children's praise presents (P)
In pairs children think of something nice about their partner, they write it down and fold it into a parcel. When both are ready, the 'presents' are exchanged, read and appreciated with a 'thank you'. This can be repeated each day in different pair groups until all pupils have been able to say something nice to each member of the class.

Praise words (P)
Brainstorm adjectives that children can apply to each other such as, kind, thoughtful, friendly, hardworking etc. The final list can be made into a poster to help them with the exercise above.

Things I like about myself (P) (can be adapted for S)
The children draw a self portrait and write (or say) three good things about themselves. For example, I am helpful, I answer questions in class, I am kind, I am good at tidying up. Older children might be encouraged at the end of each day or week to write down one or two things that they were pleased with or went well for them.

Good things books (P)
Each child makes a 'My Good Things' scrapbook. This could include positive statements about themselves or things they have done, which they can add to each day/week.

Good news roundup (P)
At the end of the day, the teacher makes some positive statements to the class about their behaviour for that day, for example: 'Kim, I noticed that you helped Harry when he hurt himself in the playground today. That was kind and helpful.' 'I saw Sarah, Jack and Jamie playing with Laura today on her first day in the class and that was very thoughtful and friendly of you all.' The class can also be invited to make positive comments about each other using the same model.

Problem solving

Children are often able to generate ideas and solutions to a problem but are not always given the opportunity. Teaching problem-solving skills helps them to understand that there can be different ways of handling difficulties and that they do have choices. This is empowering and builds confidence. It also teaches them to reflect on the consequences of various options and encourages reasoned decision making. Furthermore, children are likely to be more willing to cooperate with a solution if they have contributed to its formulation. As an activity, problem solving also promotes and validates open discussion of worries, with this being particularly important for those children who tend to keep problems to themselves. Any experiences that build confidence and a sense of empowerment are important for any child, as well as for the child who stammers. Commonly the latter will select 'teasing about stammering' as a problem to solve in therapy sessions.

Problem-solving steps

Step 1: Identify the problem, and whose problem it is.

Step 2: Brainstorm all possible solutions. Don't judge ideas at this point; the aim is to encourage creativity.

Step 3: The person whose problem it is, or the class if it's a group problem, considers each idea and the consequences of applying it. Keep the ones that seem to offer a positive outcome and cross out or erase those which wouldn't work, or would be inadvisable.

Step 4: Put the chosen solutions in order, first numbering them on the board and then writing out a separate list with the best first. Combine any that seem to be linked.

Step 5: The first solution then needs to be tried out first, within a suitable time frame, and if this doesn't work, the next one on the list can be tried.

Step 6: Keep the list of solutions handy in case the problem occurs again.

This process (see Appendix 12) helps children to tackle difficulties more independently, realise their own creativity and their ability to help others. Furthermore, motivation to comply with decisions about group problems such as 'what shall we do when the class gets too noisy' may be increased because the ideas are self-generated and 'owned'.

Activities to practise problem solving

How to get off the island (P)

In this scenario, the class is told that they are stranded on an island and they want to escape. Write the problem in the centre of the board, e.g. 'How to get off the island.' The group then brainstorms all ideas which might help their escape, without the use of any technology! The aim is to ensure that all ideas are written up and that the class is stopped from making comments about the usefulness or otherwise of any of them as this will stifle creativity. Once all ideas are on the board, the group considers which ones to keep as possibilities, which ones to delete, and finally prioritises the list of options in order of preference. This can be done as a whole group or the class can be divided up, with each group later recounting their solutions and their reasons for choosing them.

Picture problems 'What should we do?' (E, P)
Use pictures of problem situations that are familiar to the group, e.g. not being able to reach a toy in the cupboard, or being lost in a shop. Describe what has happened and ask the group what the person involved could do. Again invite lots of ideas, without evaluating them, until there are no more contributions. The various options are discussed with the children, and the consequences explored, by asking e.g. 'What might happen if he did that?' Once all ideas have been discussed, the group decides which idea to try first, and the next best etc. For older students newspaper pictures and articles that raise a number of potentially important issues for them may be used for discussion.

Real problems 'What should we do?' (E, P, S)
Describe an actual problem related to the class and ask what could be done to solve the problem. Older students may be encouraged to bring a difficult situation for the group to consider. It can take courage to contribute something personal, even when very practical; and so we have frequently started this off by asking a student speech and language therapist to contribute a real problem for a group to solve. This demonstrates that this is an effective strategy for adults as well as for children.

Example of a problem solve on teasing with a class of eight year olds

Action
  1. Tell the teacher.
  2. Talk to the dinner lady.

3. Ask one of the older children for help.
4. Say . . . yeah, so what.

See Appendix 12 for a worksheet.

Negotiation

This is a high-level communication skill which requires all the previous skills in the hierarchy. It involves having understanding of others' points of view; the ability to generate alternative ideas, present reasoned arguments; assertiveness and a readiness to compromise. Teaching students negotiation skills helps them cope more successfully with peer relationships, with parents and authority figures especially when dealing with issues that might otherwise lead to conflict.

Activities to raise awareness

Video clips (P, S)
Video-recorded examples from television programmes of good and bad negotiation are shown to the class. This is followed by a discussion of what works and why and vice versa. It is particularly helpful to identify situations when:

- Participants have rigidly opposing views and are unable to move towards a middle ground.
- One person dominates the other so that a different point of view cannot be heard.
- One person is not sufficiently assertive or has not thought their ideas through sufficiently.

This can be used to facilitate discussion about what individuals could do differently to be more effective.

Role play (P, S)
Teacher and helper role-play examples of good and bad negotiating skills to use as above.

Brainstorming
'Why is it important to be able to negotiate?'
'What skills do we need to be able to negotiate?'
(Observation, listening, turn taking, empathy, respect for others' points of view, reinforcement of others, assertiveness, preparation – having a reasoned argument in mind, flexibility.)

Discussion points
What is negotiation?
E.g. compromise, meeting in the middle, not winning or losing.

Activities for further practice

The Desert Island (P, S)
This activity is in two parts:

Part 1: Divide the class into groups of five or six pupils. The scenario presented is that the group is stranded on an island. There is fresh water and vegetation on the island but no other resources. First, each person, on their own, decides and writes down three single items that they would select to help them survive until they are rescued. Hi-tech equipment is not allowed nor ideas such as 'a year's supply of . . .' When each has chosen his or her three items, the group members are given fifteen minutes to negotiate and agree three items from their range of suggestions. At the end of this, the skills that were required to come to a joint decision are discussed and the roles that individuals took within the group are identified. For example, who seemed to take a lead, who listened to all points of view, who kept them on task? Individual goals can also be discussed at this point by asking each what they felt they were good at and whether there was anything they would like to improve upon.

Part 2: A spokesperson from each group forms a circle within the larger group. This group now negotiates a final list of three things that they will agree to take. The remainder of the class observe and each group comments on how well they feel their spokesperson negotiated on their behalf. This 'fishbowl' exercise is more challenging and the emphasis is on giving positive reinforcement to those who were spokespeople.

Summary
A framework for developing social communication skills has been presented following an established procedure which is used by a variety of groups. These have been found to be particularly effective for children and young adults who stammer, as well as for other individuals who have communication difficulties. A number of activities have been included as illustrations but these are not comprehensive.
Further exercises may be found in:
Games for Social and Life Skills (1995) by T. Bond. Cheltenham: Stanley Thornes.
Creative Drama (1987) by Sue Jennings. Oxon: Winslow Press.
Joining Together: Group Theory and Group Skills (1975) by D. Johnson and F. Johnson. New Jersey, USA: Prentice Hall.
Social Skills and the Speech Impaired (1999) by L. Rustin and A. Kuhr. London: Whurr.

Appendices: Checklists and practical exercises

Warning Bells checklist

1. Is there anyone else in the child's extended family who used to stammer?

2. Does anyone in the child's extended family still stammer?

3. Has the child been 'stammering' for more than a year?

4. Does the child have any other difficulties with speech, language or understanding?

5. Has the child had difficulties in the past with speech and language development?

What is he doing?

Is this child just hesitant or is he stammering?

Revisions e.g. 'I want a ...... some juice.' ☐

Interjections e.g. 'Can I um go outside?' ☐

Phrase repetitions e.g. 'My dog is ..... my dog is called Sam' ☐

Repeating the whole word e.g. 'But-but-but' ☐

    How many times? ☐

Repeating the first sound of the word e.g. 'C-c-c-can I?' ☐

    How many repetitions? ☐

Prolonging sounds e.g. 'Wiiiiill we ....?' ☐

Blocking sounds (mouth in position to speak but no sounds come out) ☐

Facial tension   eyes ☐   mouth ☐   other ☐

Body movements   hands ☐   feet ☐   other ☐

Disrupted breathing e.g. Gasping, speaking on incoming breath ☐

Child shows awareness

    Child says 'I can't say it' ☐

    Child gives up trying to say it ☐

    Child looks away during struggle to say it ☐

    Your instinct says child is aware ☐

    Child changes the word ☐

Situation checklist

The child stammers when he is:

Talking to himself or his toys ☐

Talking to other children ☐

Shouting ☐

Singing ☐

Explaining something to an adult ☐

Answering a question in a one to one setting with an adult ☐

Answering a question in a group ☐

Competing with other children to say something ☐

What you can do to help

- It's fine to be sympathetic

- Don't feel under pressure to say the word for him

- Ask the child what he would like you to do

- Help him to feel there's no hurry to finish
  - use more pausing
  - try to talk at the same speed as the child
  - watch your body language

- Help him to keep his language simple
  - keep your own language simple
  - use simple questions

- Encourage all the children to take turns

- Help the child develop in confidence

Rules of turn taking

- **We listen** to the speaker so that we know what they are saying and when they have finished.

- **We look** at the speaker so that we know when they are expecting us to say something (usually indicated by pausing and eye contact).

- **We wait** until the other person has completely finished even if we think we know what they are going to say.

- **Turn taking should be fair.** People should have an opportunity to have their say.

- **Don't carry on too long.** The speaker should be aware that they need to stop to let another person have their turn to talk.

Describing the stammer

Word repetitions ☐

    E.g. but but but

Number of repetitions ☐

Sound or syllable repetitions ☐

    E.g. C-c-c-c-can I?

Number of repetitions ☐

Prolonging sounds ☐

    E.g. wiiiiiiiil we

Blocking sounds ☐

    (mouth in position but no sound)

Facial tension

    eyes ☐

    mouth ☐

    other ☐

Body movements

    head ☐

    hands ☐

    feet ☐

    other ☐

Disrupted breathing ☐

    E.g. gasping, talking on incoming breath

Awareness

    Says 'I can't say it' ☐

    Gives up trying to say it ☐

    Looks away during struggle to say it ☐

    Your instinct says he is aware ☐

Avoidance

    Changes words ☐

    Avoids words ☐

    Avoids situations ☐

    Uses fillers ☐

    Concealing stammer ☐

When is he stammering?

When he is talking to himself ☐

When he shouts ☐

When he sings ☐

When he is talking to his class teacher ☐

    explaining something ☐

    answering a question ☐

    competing with other children to answer ☐

    other teachers and school staff, e.g. lunchtime assistants ☐

    the head teacher ☐

When he is reading aloud

    in a one to one setting with the teacher ☐

    in a small group setting ☐

    in front of the class ☐

    in front of the school (e.g. assembly) ☐

When he is talking to children informally ☐

When he is talking in a small group of children ☐

When he is talking in front of the class ☐

When he is talking in front of the school ☐

When he answers the register ☐

When he takes messages to other members of staff ☐

When he is being told off ☐

When he seems excited ☐

© Rustin *et al.* (2001) *Stammering*. David Fulton Publishers

The cycle of stammering

The way a person *thinks* affects how he *feels*, which alters his *physical* state and therefore his *behaviour* (Beck 1976)

This cycle explains how a child's stammering may fluctuate according to how he feels and the situation he is in. The cycle may be positive or negative in its effects.

Example of a negative cycle. A child is asked to read aloud in front of his class. If he thinks other children might laugh at him, this may make him anxious and embarrassed. These feelings may make him physically tense which could increase his stammering, thereby realising his fears, and perpetuating the negative cycle:

THINKING
'They will laugh when I stammer'

BEHAVIOUR
stammering, avoidance

FEELINGS
embarrassment, anxiety

PHYSICAL
tension, 'butterflies'

Example of a positive cycle: If the child thinks that even if children do laugh, it's just them being silly, this makes him feel stronger and more confident. These feelings make him physically more relaxed which helps him to be more fluent, thereby confirming his position of strength and perpetuating the positive cycle:

THINKING
'The children who laugh
are being silly'

BEHAVIOUR
more fluency

FEELINGS
more confidence

PHYSICAL
relaxed

© Rustin *et al.* (2001) *Stammering*. David Fulton Publishers

To my teacher _____ (teacher's name)

From _____ (name)

I want to tell you this about my problem with talking

I want to tell you this about me

When I am having trouble talking, I would like you to

When I am having trouble talking, it doesn't help when

Things I do so that people won't know about my problem

How my life would be different if I didn't have this problem

General checklist for whole class

Do you think that pupils are teased or bullied in this school?   Yes ☐   No ☐

If the answer is 'Yes', do you think teachers are aware of it?   Yes ☐   No ☐

Have you ever been laughed at?   Yes ☐   No ☐

          called unkind names?   Yes ☐   No ☐

          mimicked?   Yes ☐   No ☐

          threatened?   Yes ☐   No ☐

          deliberately hit/kicked/hurt?   Yes ☐   No ☐

Would you tell your teacher if someone teased/bullied you?   Yes ☐   No ☐

Would you tell your parents?   Yes ☐   No ☐

Do you have any suggestions for what the teacher could do about teasing and bullying?

I want to tell you what happened to me

This is how I have been teased or bullied
(It's OK to use the exact words that were said)

This is how I reacted

This is what happened next

This is how the teasing/bullying made me feel

This is what I would like to be done about it

Any other comments

Problem-solving worksheet

1: Identify the problem.   2: Brainstorm the solutions.   3: Think about the consequences of each one.   4: Choose the best ideas.   5: Put them in the order you would like to try them out.   6: Have a go!

My problem is

Action   1:

2:

3:

4:

Useful addresses

The Michael Palin Centre for Stammering Children
Finsbury Health Centre
Pine Street
London ECIR OLP
Tel: (020) 7530 4238
Fax: (020) 7833 3842
Email: *arsc@dial.pipex.com*

The British Stammering Association
15 Old Ford Road
London E2 9PJ
Tel: (020) 8983 1003
Fax: (020) 8983 3591
Helpline: (0845) 603 2001
Email: *mail@stammering.org*

The Royal College of Speech and Language Therapists
2 White Hart Yard,
London SE1 1NX
Tel: (020) 7378 1200
Fax: (020) 7403 7254
Email: *postmaster@rcslt.org*

References

Ambrose, N. G. *et al.* (1993) 'Genetic aspects of early childhood stuttering', *Journal of Speech and Hearing Research* **36**, 701–706.

Ambrose, N. G., and Yairi, E. (1994) 'The development of awareness of stuttering in pre-school children', *Journal of Fluency Disorders* **19**, 229–46.

Andrews, G. *et al.* (1983) 'Stuttering: A review of research findings and theories circa 1982', *Journal of Speech and Hearing Disorders* **48**, 226–46.

Beck, A. T. (1976) *Cognitive Therapy and the Emotional Disorders*. New York: International Universities Press.

Bernstein-Ratner, N. E. (1997) 'Stuttering: A Psycholinguistic Perspective', in Curlee, R. and Siegel, G. (eds) *Nature and Treatment of Stuttering: New Directions* (2nd edn, pp. 99–127). Boston: Allyn and Bacon.

Birdwhistell. R. (1970) *Kinetics and Context*. Philadelphia: University of Pennsylvania Press.

Bloodstein, O. (1995) *A Handbook on Stuttering*. San Diego, CA: Singular Publishing.

Caruso, A. J. *et al.* (1995) 'Emotional arousal and stuttering: the impact of cognitive stress', in Starkweather, C. W. and Peters, H. F. M. (eds) *Stuttering: Proceedings of the First World Congress on Fluency Disorders*. Nijmegen, The Netherlands: International Fluency Association.

Cullinan, W. L. and Springer, M. T. (1980) 'Voice initiation times in stuttering and non stuttering children', *Journal of Speech and Hearing Research* **23**, 344–60.

Curlee, R. (1993) 'Identification and management of beginning stuttering', in Curlee, R. (ed.) *Stuttering and Related Disorders of Fluency* (pp. 1–22). New York:Thieme Medical Publishers.

Curlee, R and Siegel, G. (eds) (1997) *Nature and Treatment of Stuttering: New Directions* (2nd edn). Boston: Allyn and Bacon.

De Nil, L. (1999) 'Stuttering: a neurophysiologic perspective', in Bernstein-Ratner, N. and Healey, E. C. (eds) *Stuttering Research and Practice: Bridging the Gap* (pp. 85–102). Mahwah, NJ: Lawrence Erlbaum.

DfEE (1997) *Excellence for all Children*. London: HMSO.

DfEE (2000) *Provision of Speech and Language Therapy Services to Children with Special Educational Needs*. London: HMSO.

Faber, A. and Mazlish, E. (1980) *How to Talk so Kids will Listen and Listen so Kids will Talk*. Avon Books: New York.

Guitar, B. (1998) *Stuttering: An Integrated Approach to its Nature and Treatment* (2nd edn). Baltimore: Williams and Wilkins.

Horsley, I. A. and Fitzgibbon, C. T. (1987) 'Stuttering children: investigation of a stereotype', *British Journal of Disorders of Communication* **22**(1), 19–35.

Howell, P. *et al.* (1999) 'Exchange of stuttering from function words to content words with age', *Journal of Speech, Language, and Hearing Research* **42**, 345–54.

Kidd, K. K. *et al.* (1978) 'The possible causes of the sex ratio in stuttering and its implications', *Journal of Fluency Disorders* **3**, 13–23.

Kloth, S. A. M. *et al.* (1998) 'Communicative styles of mothers interacting with their preschool children: A factor analytic study', *Journal of Child Language* **25**, 149–68.

Kloth, S. A. M. *et al.* (1999) 'Persistence and remission of incipient stuttering among high-risk children', *Journal of Fluency Disorders* **24**, 253–65.

Langlois, A. and Long, S. H. (1988) 'A model for teaching parents to facilitate fluent speech', *Journal of Fluency Disorders* **13**, 163–72.

Lees, R. M. (1999) 'Stammering children in school', in McCartney, E. (ed.) *Speech/Language Therapists and Teachers Working Together*. London: Whurr.

Lees, R. M. (2000) 'It takes two to stammer', in MacKay, G. and Anderson, C. (eds) *Pragmatic Difficulties of Communication*. London: David Fulton.

Logan, K. J. and Conture, E. G., (1995) 'Length, grammatical complexity and rate differences in stuttered and fluent conversational utterances of children who stutter', *Journal of Fluency Disorders* **20**, 35–61.

Matthews, S. *et al.* (1997) 'Parent-child interaction therapy and dysfluency: A single case study', *European Journal of Disorders of Communication* **32**, 1244–59.

Meyers, S. and Freeman, F. (1985a) 'Interruptions as a variable in stuttering and dysfluency', *Journal of Speech and Hearing Research* **28**, 428–35.

Meyers, S. and Freeman, F. (1985b) 'Are mothers of stutterers different? An investigation of social-communicative inter-actions', *Journal of Fluency Disorders* **10**, 193–209.

Miller, S. (1993) Multiple measures of anxiety and psycho-physiologic arousal in stutterers and nonstutterers during nonspeech and speech tasks of increasing complexity. Unpublished doctoral dissertation, University of Texas at Dallas.

Mooney, S. and Smith, P. K (1994) 'Bullying and the child who stammers', *British Journal of Special Education* **22**, 24–7.

Nierman, R. N. *et al.* (1994) 'Relation between phonologic difficulty and the occurrence of dysfluencies in the early stage of stuttering', *Journal of Speech and Hearing Research* **37**, 504–509.

Nippold, M. A. and Rudzinski, M. (1995) 'Parents' speech and children's stuttering: a critique of the literature', *Journal of Speech and Hearing Research* **38**, 978–89.

Onslow, M. (1993) *Behavioral Management of Stuttering*. London: Singular Publishing Group.

Onslow, M. *et al.* (1994) 'A control/experimental trial of an operant treatment for early stuttering', *Journal of Speech and Hearing Research* **37**, 1244–59.

Onslow, M. and Packman, A. (eds) (1999) *The Handbook of Early Stuttering Intervention*. San Diego, CA: Singular Publishing Group.

Oyler, M. E. and Ramig, P. R. (1995) 'Vulnerability in Stuttering Children'. Paper presented at the Annual Convention of the American Speech-Language-Hearing Association, Orlando, Florida.

Paden, P. E. *et al.* (1999) 'Early childhood stuttering II: Initial status of phonological abilities', *Journal of Speech, Language, and Hearing Research* **42**, 1113–24.

Peters, H. F. M. and Starkweather, C. W. (1990) 'The interaction between speech motor coordination and language processes in the development of stuttering', *Journal of Fluency Disorders* **15**, 115–25.

Rustin, L. (1987) *Assessment and Therapy Programme for Dysfluent Children*. Windsor: NFER-Nelson

Rustin, L. *et al.* (1995) *The Management of Stuttering in Adolescence: a communication skills approach*. London: Whurr Publishers.

Rustin, L. *et al.* (1996) *Assessment and Therapy Programme for Dysfluent Children*. London: Whurr Publishers.

Rustin, L. and Kuhr, A. (1999) *Social skills and the Speech Impaired* (2nd edn). London: Whurr Publishers.

Seider, R. A. *et al.* (1983) 'Recovery and persistence of stuttering among relatives of stutterers', *Journal of Speech and Hearing Disorders* **48**, 402–409.

Starkweather, C. W. (1987) *Fluency and Stuttering.* Englewood Cliffs, NJ: Prentice-Hall.

Starkweather, C. W. and Givens-Ackerman, J. (1997) *Stuttering: PRO-ED Studies in Communicative Disorders.* Austin, Texas: PRO-ED Inc.

Starkweather, C. W. and Gottwald, S. R. (1990) 'The demands and capacities model II: clinical applications', *Journal of Fluency Disorders* **15**, 143–58.

Starkweather, C. W. and Gottwald, S. R. (1993) 'A pilot study of relations among specific measures obtained at intake and discharge in a program of prevention and early intervention for stuttering', *Journal of Speech-Language Pathology* **2**, 51–8.

Starkweather, C. W. and Myers, M. (1979) 'Duration of subsegments within the intervocalic interval in stutterers and non stutterers', *Journal of Fluency Disorders* **4**, 205–14.

Stephenson-Opsal, D. and Bernstein-Ratner, N. (1988) 'Maternal speech rate modification and childhood stuttering', *Journal of Fluency Disorders* **15**, 175–243.

Stewart, T. and Turnbull, J. (1995) *Working with Dysfluent Children: Practical Approaches to Assessment and Therapy.* Oxford: Winslow Press.

Till, J. A. *et al.* (1983) 'Phonatory and manual reaction times of stuttering and non-stuttering children', *Journal of Speech and Hearing Research* **26**, 171–80.

Wall, M. J. *et al.* (1981) 'Influences on stuttering in young child stutterers', *Journal of Fluency Disorders* **6**, 283–98.

Watkins, R. V. *et al.* (1999) 'Early childhood stuttering III: Initial status of expressive language abilities', *Journal of Speech, Language, and Hearing Research* **42**, 1125–35.

Weber, C. and Smith, A. (1990) 'Autonomic correlates of stuttering and speech assessed in a range of experimental tasks', *Journal of Speech and Hearing Research* **33**, 690–706.

Yairi, E. and Ambrose, N. (1992) 'Onset of stuttering in preschool children: selected factors', *Journal of Speech and Hearing Research* **35**, 782–8.

Yairi, E. *et al.* (1996) 'Genetics of stuttering: a critical review', *Journal of Speech and Hearing Research* **39**, 771–84.

Yairi, E. *et al.* (1996) 'Predictive factors of persistence and recovery', *Journal of Communication Disorders* **29**, 51–77.

Yaruss, J. S. (1999) 'Utterance length, syntactic complexity and childhood stuttering', *Journal of Speech, Language, and Hearing Research* **42**, 329–44.

Zimmerman, G. N. (1980) 'Stuttering: a disorder of movement', *Journal of Speech and Hearing Research* **23**, 122–36.

Index